FOREST REGIONS OF THE UNITED STATES

TREES & FORESTS OF AMERICA

TREES

& FORESTS

OF AMERICA

PHOTOGRAPHS AND TEXT BY Tim Palmer

ABRAMS, NEW YORK

In memory of Doug Finlayson, who loved trees, forests, and photography

Page 1
CHESTNUT and WHITE OAKS,
Humpback Rocks, Virginia

Pages 2–3
OAKS, HICKORIES, and VIRGINIA PINES,
Blue Ridge Parkway, Virginia

Pages 4–5
DOUGLAS-FIRS,
Skamania Lodge, Washington

Left
PONDEROSA PINES and DOUGLAS-FIRS,
Ochoco Mountains, Oregon

CONTENTS

THE WAY TO THE WOODS

I DID NOT HAVE to go far. It took me only a minute to run down a path and through a field of goldenrod to the edge of the woods. School was out. I was alone. I felt wild and free.

The deep forest awaiting me was adorned with everything I called "nature." Untold, indescribable wonders lured me in. I parted the hanging branches that caught and absorbed the full force of afternoon sunlight at the boundary of the woods, and I stepped inside. The shade came suddenly and completely, and as my pupils dilated to take in more light, my mind and spirit did the same.

Once inside the forest, I walked slowly, my feet pressing the ground softly, silently. A new coolness washed across my face, and, far above, a breeze fluttered the leaves of tall maple trees. That heavenly rustling was the only noise, prompting me to stop, to stand utterly still, and to listen closer until I heard the distant trill of a bird—the quick, melodious scale of a hermit thrush, which I knew as a song of the forest.

I hadn't given a thought to what might happen next. For the time being, I simply wanted to see what there was to see. The green of it all was so vibrant that it suffused the light itself. From groundcover to upper canopy, the color alone soothed and comforted me. But at the same time, other aspects of the woods excited me. Fallen logs challenged me to jump over or to walk their lengths, the way one might do on a balance beam, just for fun.

This forest behind our house was my escape, my training ground, and my own private world. As a child, I went there often, and the trees screened out the nearby houses and the roads the way a closed curtain might. But behind that curtain, I found an endlessly intriguing world. Why did the locust trees grow at the edge of the woods, and the hemlocks deep inside? Why did I find more squirrels in white oak trees than in red oaks?

In a few places, sunshine filtered through the branches with visible, elegant shafts of light that illuminated something fundamentally correct and peaceable about life. I didn't really know what it was, and I certainly didn't have words for it, but even at a young age I realized that I had found a certain satisfaction in the woods that had been missing everywhere else.

Like many other people who discover the allure of forests lying just behind their houses, at the local park, or out past the grid of town, I have long regarded trees as symbols of the natural world. As I learned more about trees, their lives became a testament to the forces of both creation and decay. They came to embody powerful connections between earth and sky, wilderness and civilization, life and death.

We breathe the oxygen that trees produce; these magnificent organisms literally expire the fuel for our blood, the life force for our bodies. To state this important fact another way: We inhale what trees exhale, and vice versa, and it's difficult to imagine a relationship more interdependent and intimate than that.

The fibrous soil of wild forests protects the land from erosion and minimizes the hardships of droughts and hazards of floods by sponging up rainfall and then releasing water slowly. In a healthy forest, tree roots and the underground ecosystem surrounding them make the soil not only stable, but also fertile and productive by processing nitrogen and other essential elements and by hosting insects and microbes by the billions. This eclectic community is essential in order for the earth beneath our feet to support the greater food chain—from microbes, to plants, to animals.

Woodlands are essential habitats for whole communities of wild creatures that would simply die without trees. As keystone species that many other life-forms depend upon, trees offer food and shelter. They make the rest of life possible.

Medicines originally derived from plants, microbes, and animals in forests account for 40 percent of all commercial drugs. Among these is Taxol, a treatment for cancer, originally found only in yew trees of the West Coast. We use trees to make paper, houses, furniture, tools, and countless other objects. The continuous supply of trees for all those uses depends on healthy forests, and therefore on entire ecosystems—soil, air, water, organisms—that produce the trees. They don't just live in isolation.

Forests cool our hot days with their shade and shelter us from the wind, which might howl overhead but can scarcely be felt behind a line of flexible trunks, buffering branches, and

REDWOODS and sunrise, northern California
Through a wisp of morning fog, the sun beams down on redwoods and Pacific rhododendron at Del Norte Coast Redwoods State Park. Taller than all other trees, redwoods need summertime moisture provided by fog, and they grow only along the coasts of California and southern Oregon.

RED FIR and MOUNTAIN HEMLOCK, **Anderson Peak, California**
Flourishing at high elevations that extend almost to timberline, these trees are well adapted to heavy snow loads here in the Sierra Nevada south of Donner Pass.

AUTUMN LEAVES, **Ricketts Glen, Pennsylvania**
Wet leaves of a red and yellow sugar maple, golden-brown American beech, and finely toothed yellow birch shine and color the landscape even after the rain has pummeled them down onto sandstone slabs beneath a canopy of northern hardwoods. About two dozen species of trees account for most of the outstanding autumn color in the East.

quivering leaves. Trees sequester atmospheric carbon that is in troubling oversupply because we burn oil, gas, and coal at rates that are causing the entire planet to heat up like a poorly vented greenhouse. Planting trees and letting them grow is one of the essential steps toward alleviating the ominous problem of global warming.

Beyond our practical needs for trees, many of us yearn all our lives for the comforting refuge of the forest. When we go for walks we go to the woods, whether in the Olympic rainforest or in Central Park in New York City. We enjoy trees so much that if they don't exist we plant them in our lawns and along our streets, even if we have to pump precious water for them and dutifully rake fallen leaves over and over each autumn. Trees make our communities and countrysides beautiful in ways that are central to their livability, and I believe that this beauty is essential to a positive outlook on the world.

More than any other natural feature, trees determine how a landscape looks to us—the humid green empire of deciduous forests in the East, dark boggy depths of the North Woods, parklands of conifers in the West, savannas of oaks brightening California, and cathedral groves of firs towering in the Northwest. Forests may be the most beloved part of the American landscape.

IN THIS BOOK, I'D like to show you trees and forests I have known. I've gone out to the woods that lie all across America and gotten lost there—not by failing to find my way out, but by forgetting, for awhile, that the rest of the world exists. With a sense of total engagement, I sought out remarkable places that still show the beauty of nature. Through the transparent lenses of my camera, I'd like to take you to these forests that I've explored in the drama of all seasons—in the shrouds of snowfall and rainstorm as well as in the exuberant clarity of sunny days.

These images of towering canopy overhead and slippery root underfoot, of cool green photosynthesis and warm multicolored rot, have all heartened me in a troubled world because all these scenes indicate—quite simply—the triumph of life. They signify nature in the ways it has nourished the world since the beginning of time. The need for that nourishment is not likely to change very much, even though our technologies and cultures change a great deal.

With my camera, I have attempted to capture images of nature as it exists. I used film that records the colors of the natural world in a realistic way, and I did not alter the color or the content of the photos by digital or other means after I took them. Knowing that nature is already filtering the light I see, I avoided the use of lens filters except for an occasional graduated gray overlay to darken a white sky that would otherwise underexpose the rest of the picture. I used no artificial light. Many photographers now alter their photos in seductive ways that certainly make their pictures more amazing and more sensational—though less realistic. Finding no fault with this, I consider myself not so much an artist but simply a messenger for the natural world. I hope to show the earth as it is—to simply convey an art form that already exists. I do this with the modest goal of inspiring others to go out and see these wondrous landscapes for themselves, and to be as thrilled with the reality of what they find as I am.

I took pictures of scenes that anyone can go out and see. However, these photos are not the result of random walks in the woods. I searched for the greatest beauty I could find in every forest I visited. And I, of course, have my own ideas of what beauty is. For example, I am unabashedly fond of big trees and am drawn to them as if to some magic moment in my distant and formative past. But I also believe that diminutive trees such as dogwoods—with their delicate upturned branches and full-bodied blossoms—are just as beautiful.

Beyond beauty and variety, I also looked for visual cues that helped me to understand life in the woods. One image might show how a red fir accommodates a lot of snow; another might illustrate the effects of fire or a forest's recovery from it. I searched for native trees; this book is about nature and wildness and exotic plants introduced from other parts of the globe that often cause problems for the native life. Therefore you will find no eucalyptus or banyan in this book, remarkable as those trees might be.

Systematically, I sought out many different species of trees in all regions of the country, but my journey was also an intensely personal one, and I can only hope that those who read this book will be heartened by what I have seen.

Though my photos are entirely realistic, they are not representative of what I found in forests across America. This is because I sought natural and wild forests in places affected as little as possible by the changes wrought during the past few centuries. Though trees of some kind can be found almost everywhere, wild or truly natural areas have become rare in today's world. Many of my pictures were taken in state or national parks, wilderness areas, or nature reserves, though

BALDCYPRESS TREES, Lumber River, North Carolina
Inundated with river water for much of the year, baldcypresses grace the wetlands of the Southeast and send up protruding "knees" that may help to stabilize the tall trees in their flooded habitat. Water tupelos with new green leaves share this productive but demanding riparian niche in the ecosystem.

BLACK TUPELO, Gathland State Park, Maryland
In the first light of dawn, an unusually tall black tupelo reaches for sunlight while new leaves of the Appalachian's mixed broadleaf forest unfurl in early May. Many birds and mammals eat the tupelos' fleshy fruits.

SWEETGUM and RED MAPLE, Tallulah Gorge, Georgia

Starry leaves of sweetgums and sharply toothed red maples paint a brilliant scene in autumn. Gray bedrock beneath these trees steps down in a steep gorge to the Chattooga River.

SYCAMORE in snowstorm, northern Pennsylvania
Heavy, wet snow fills the atmosphere during a winter storm along the Clarion River. Sycamores specialize in riverfront or riparian locations where they stabilize erosion-prone banks, tap ever-present water supplies, cope with the hazards of floods, and tolerate thick new deposits of silt.

these represent only about 10 percent of our land. The fact that I needed to go to these enclaves in order to capture scenes of native America indicates how important the protected reserves truly are. No less, it indicates the urgency of expanding those reserves and of better managing forests elsewhere so that our woodlands can provide us with the myriad benefits of nature, which I describe in some detail later in this book.

In chapter one, I reflect on the quiet art of seeing the forest, and on the purposeful passion that accompanies me to the woods, this time not as a child who entered a magical realm behind a curtain of green foliage, but as an adult with a sense of discovery that has endured the years and the changes that life inevitably brings. In chapter two, I explore the workings of a tree and question how these amazing organisms do what they do: germinating from the tiniest seeds; making solid bulwarks of life with nothing but air and water plus a pinch of soil; dying quiet or tumultuous deaths when their final days arrive, then recycling themselves into vigorous new generations. Chapter three broadens this topic to cover whole forests—how trees interact with one another and with all that lies around them, how they support virtually every form of wildlife you might name, and how they protect our soil, water, and air. Chapter four—where most of the photos in this book appear—features a nationwide tour, with pictures from each of the great woodland biomes. In chapter five, I write about what is happening to our forests, and why we simply cannot afford to take them for granted.

To take the photos for this book, I immersed myself in America's forests, inhaled the piney terpenes and sweetly rotting aromas of real life, planted my boots into rooted soil, and climbed the steep ladders of branches halfway to the sky. I kicked my feet as I walked through piles of orange leaves in autumn. I tracked woodland creatures in the freshly fallen snow of winter. I celebrated the yellow-green bursting of spring—a hopeful season that promises new life and immortality, not to individuals even as ancient as the four-thousand-year-old bristlecone pines, but to the greater system of life.

I invite you to step into these forests that I have explored, and to share with me in the life and the abundance all around us. Most of all, I invite you to step into your own woods and discover the wonders of nature that we are all entitled to inherit.

FREMONT COTTONWOODS, Patagonia, Arizona
On a mid-winter evening, a full moon creeps up from the horizon behind a grove of cottonwoods along Sonoita Creek, near the Mexican border. Even in the desert, these massive trees manage to get the water they need alongside streams so long as the flows are not diverted. Cottonwoods serve as keystone species—many other plants and animals depend on them.

DOUGLAS-FIRS with TANOAKS, Humbug Mountain State Park, Oregon
Seen during a brief reprieve between winter storms, fresh snow covers a young forest of Douglas-firs, with small tanoaks in the center. Protected by the forest around them, these trees brace against heavy winds at the summit of the second-highest mountain that rises directly from the ocean on the coast of Oregon.

PONDEROSA PINE and DOUGLAS-FIRS, **Siskiyou Summit, Oregon**
At a biologically intriguing intersection of differing climates and geographies, the Siskiyou Mountains in southern Oregon and northern California support more conifer species than any other place in the world. Here, for a brief moment, the setting sun breaks through multiple layers of clouds that had been hiding the wonders of this great forest under thick layers of moisture.

TANOAKS and CALIFORNIA-BAYS, **Big Sur, California**
Plentiful tanoaks and California-bays with sharply pungent leaves thrive along the West Coast, seen here in the morning when cool, moist air wafts in from the Pacific Ocean at Julia Pfeiffer Burns State Park.

SAGUARO CACTI, San Pedro Valley, Arizona

Even though their trunks are not made of solid wood, saguaro cacti manage to stand tall in the Sonoran Desert. Pleats in the fluted stems swell outward as the cacti opportunistically suck-up water following infrequent rainstorms. Small trees are the blue palo verde, whose green bark and twigs help to photosynthesize and produce food in the absence of large leaves, which would never survive the desert's desiccating aridity.

COCONUT PALMS, island of Hawaii
Rustled by soft tropical winds blowing off the Pacific, coconut palms have served Hawaiians well with food since the early Polynesians first brought this tree to the islands many centuries ago.

GOFF WOODS, Ohio
In a small but exquisite grove near Lake Erie, an eastern cottonwood rises on the left, a red oak in the center, and tuliptrees to the right and in the background. Much of the Midwest was once covered with this type of lush, deciduous forest.

FOXTAIL PINES, Kearsarge Pass, California
Weathering sub-zero cold, heavy snowpacks, fearsome winds, prolonged droughts, and other challenges of high elevation in the Sierra Nevada, foxtail pines with their distinctive golden bark endure the ages in elegant style.

Overleaf: SUGAR MAPLES, Nerstrand Woods, Minnesota
Sugar maples filter morning light in Nerstrand-Big Woods State Park, south of Minneapolis—one of the finest stands of old-growth forest left in the Midwest.

CHAPTER ONE

ARBOREAL VISIONS OF WILD AMERICA

Do we ever not see trees?

Go outside. Look around.

In rural America—and in most of our cities and suburban neighborhoods as well—you'll likely see trees. They tower over the rest of the biological world almost everywhere—from New England, where sugar maples crown front and back yards, to southern California where fan palms rise in lush oases. Even on the Great Plains or in the desert, a tree of some kind often rises within view.

We look at trees all the time. But do we really notice them?

Each of us might go to the woods for different reasons, but when I went there to take pictures for this book, I simply wanted to *see*. So here at the outset I'd like to reflect a bit on what it's like to do this thing that's so common, yet amazing.

The first challenge is that, indeed, one can't see the forest for the trees. This is because the forest is *made* of trees, and some block the view of others. Low limbs angle at eye level, and the foliage of the young clutters the foreground when I strive to see the trunk of a revered elder rising in the back. Vigorous shrubs and vines including poison ivy hang in front of the view I want to cleanly capture on film. And that's just the beginning of the visual and logistical complexity in many of the woodlands of America; the forest is infinitely more than a stand of trees obscured by other trees. A forest is a garden, a habitat, a system of life, a whole geography, and so it's impossible to truly see the whole thing at any one time.

Both the familiar simplicity and the mind-numbing complexity of trees can easily blind me to their actual shapes, to their true natures, and to their unique beauty. So, when I look at trees and forests, I try to look through the chaos and find patterns. For example, three large trunks in a row or a whole stand bent leeward from the wind might catch my eye. I watch for vivid colors—not just autumn foliage, but the gold of old bark on pines, the red of dogwood berries, and the lemon-green of vanilla leaf covering the ground. I look for points of focus—perhaps the very top of the tree, or maybe the place where a large limb joins the trunk, like an arm to a body. I try to see the whole forest in its infinite complexity, and I also try to see pieces as small as a seed, which might be barely visible but ready to grow.

As much as I try to simply see one thing, I'm faced with the reality that everything is connected, especially in nature, and so one sight takes me to another, and another, and my stack of photos gets larger and larger.

I search for the exquisite, and when I find it, I first pause, then admire, and then wonder about the unfathomable power and abundance of beauty wherever the natural world survives. This beauty is also evident in mountains, rivers, seashores, grasslands, and deserts, and it evokes wonderment wherever I see it. But to me, a certain basic beauty is nowhere more evident than in trees and forests. They are, after all, among our most obvious indicators of life, representing knowledge, spirit, and immortality—from the Garden of Eden described so long ago, to a grove of maples that still shades a Pennsylvania hillside where my ancestors lie in rest.

Like others, I look to any landscape with certain ingrained expectations. When I close my eyes and think "forest," I imagine tall columns of mature trees in the Appalachians, big boles towering upward to a dome overhead—a virtual sky of its own. I might also think of the brilliant autumn foliage of maples, basswoods, or beeches when they are backlit by the sun as it beams toward the heart of the New England forest in October. Winter follows the fall, and so my memory shifts to Sierra Nevada forests where, exploring in the snow, I've found welcome refuge by taking off my skis and crawling beneath drooping branches of the white fir, which often reach to the ground and have sheltered me from severe blizzards.

I imagine these kinds of forests, but I also go to the woods with an open mind, and I look for surprises. I save room in my day for unanticipated scenes. For example, I had never expected to be impressed by the lowly sumac, but then one autumn day I crawled on all fours into a grove of these diminutive trees, and I had never seen them so red, so elegant, so improbably decorative, with radial fans of arcing compound leaves creating an entire forest canopy a mere five feet off the ground. Not until then did I realize that the little sumac is truly an amazing tree.

In deeper woods, the sight of an aged hemlock that happened to catch an errant ray of glowing sunlight sent me grabbing for my camera and tripod, digging impatiently into my pack for the

Reflection of DOUGLAS-FIRS, Cascade Mountains, Oregon
Shimmering as an abstract reflection in the McKenzie River, a riparian forest shades this quiet stream front.

STAGHORN SUMAC near Westfield, Massachusetts
Autumn is the time of extraordinary forest color, especially in the Northeast and northern Midwest. At the edge of an overgrown field, this staghorn sumac flames red in early October.

HARDWOODS at Green Lakes State Park, New York
Sugar maples and tuliptrees reflect morning light in an eastern old-growth forest just outside the city of Syracuse and offer a hint of the fascinating complexity in the species-rich central hardwoods region.

Overleaf: RED MAPLE and TULIPTREES, Ohiopyle, Pennsylvania
With a rare, bird's-eye view to the tall canopy of the Appalachian forest, this photo at tree top level was taken from a railroad bridge that's now used as a bicycle trail in Ohiopyle State Park.

best among seven lenses I carry, and hustling with my shutter-release cable before the light—so splendid but so ephemeral—was gone. Then, after a sigh when the picture was taken, and after a gratifying feeling that I had seized a truly special moment from the uncompromising passage of time, the same scene imparted on me one final and insatiable desire: I wished that what I took home on film could be just half as exhilarating, half as satisfying, half as life affirming as the tree and the forest that I actually saw.

My own view of the beauty of trees rests upon a cultural view that has changed through history.

The earliest white settlers in America were both awed and cowed by the immensity of the forest confronting them. William Bradford, the Pilgrims' journalist and governor, wrote in the mid-1600s of a "hideous and desolate wilderness" beyond the recently built stockade of his town. It was, above all else, a wilderness of trees.

With Bradford's voice ringing out, three hundred years of nearly untempered assault on America's forests ensued. In most of the East, South, Midwest, and Great Plains, all the original forests were cut, and the forests of the West were treated scarcely better. Trees impeded farming, and logging was regarded as the work that built the nation. Paul Bunyan became a mythical hero of outsized proportions. For most people, a wild, natural forest was seen not for what it was but for what it could become—lumber, furniture, houses.

Yet trees, if not whole forests, maintained a certain privileged status—a lingering reverence going back, perhaps, to Druid times for us of Irish and western European descent, or to similar connections with nature in other cultures. Singular large trees, in certain places, were respected even while every other log was hauled away on wagons and later on trucks and trains. Connecticut settlers hid the charter to their colony in a large oak when King James II demanded that it be returned in 1687; the Charter Oak's death was widely mourned nearly two hundred years later. The Louis Vieux Elm, on the plains of Kansas, gained fame for shading pioneer campsites on the Oregon Trail and remains, at this writing, with only a sprig of life. Other communities had similar trees, some of them celebrated in myth, poem, and song. Peace councils were held under spreading limbs.

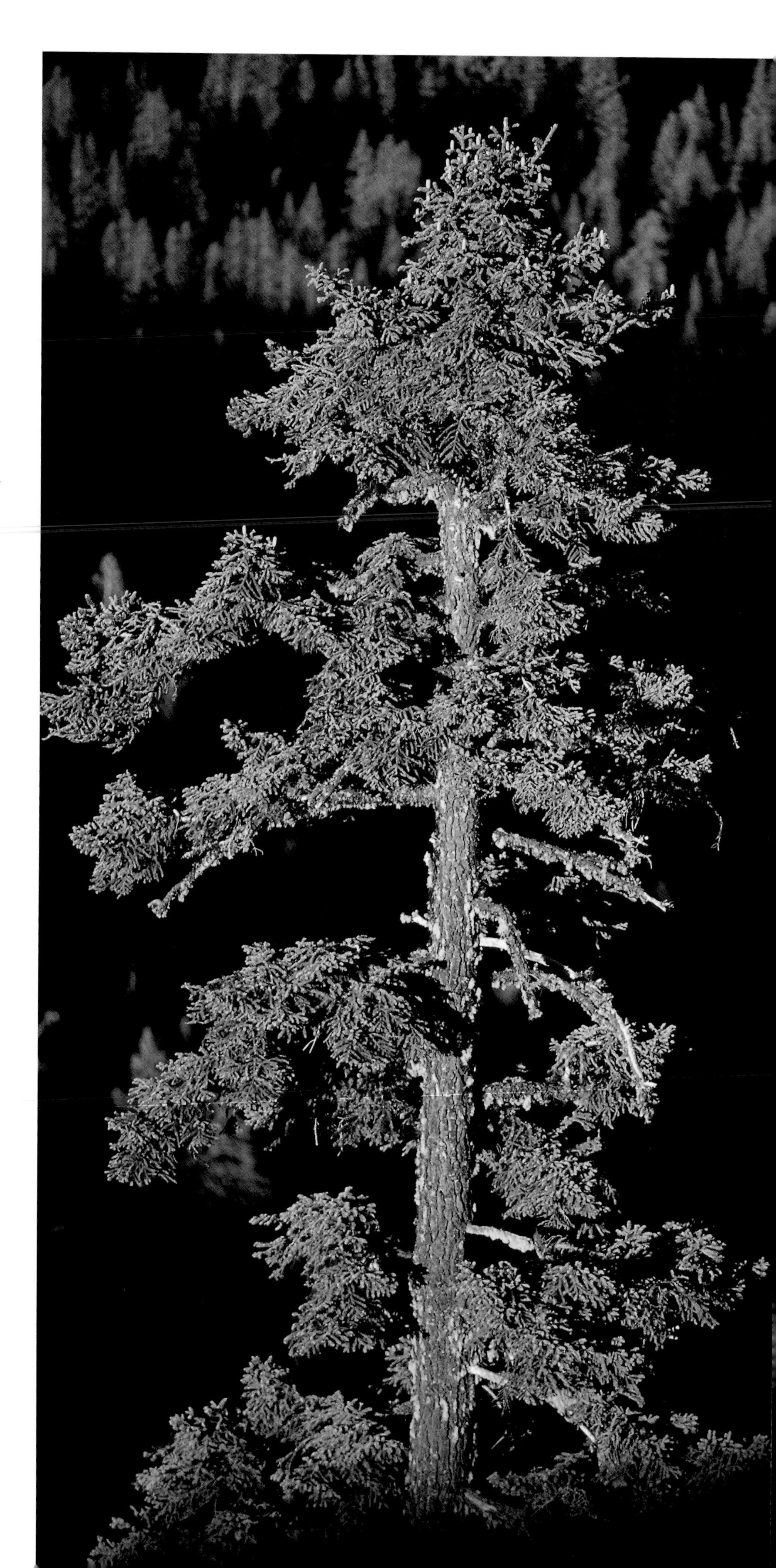

OAK TREES at sunrise near Asheville, North Carolina
Sunrise burns through a ridgetop of red and white oaks along with a few shortleaf pines in the southern Appalachian Mountains.

SHASTA RED FIR, Marble Mountains, California
While the shape and stature of individual trees are often obscured by the thick tangle of everything else in a forest, this uncommon fir stood alone in the glow of sunset on its rocky but wind-sheltered perch high in the Klamath River basin.

Agreements were signed. Picnics were eaten. Lovers no doubt met, and couples were married under favored trees.

Even as logging swept westward like a breaking wave and the paradigm of rapidly liquidating natural wealth reigned unchallenged, a few tracts of old trees were preserved. Forests were set aside in Pennsylvania at Cook Forest, in Minnesota at Nerstrand Woods, and in California at the Bidwell estate. Some groves were spared by the timber barons themselves, with credit given to an aging patriarch who, after leveling everything else he owned, bequeathed a few hundred acres to the public along with a sentiment that the next generation should know that America was once something more than a field of stumps. We've long held a conflicted aesthetic—a belief that trees are beautiful even if we think lumber is more important and profitable.

When President Benjamin Harrison signed a bill in 1890 primarily for protection of forests at Sequoia National Park, a new precedent was set to protect our nation's most extraordinary woodlands. The trees were spared for their natural value (one year later Harrison also reserved the first lands that would become national forests). Tourists flocked to the giant sequoia grove simply to *see* trees of such grandeur.

Protection of New York's six million-acre Adirondack State Park in 1892 marked a further awakening to the importance of undisturbed forests as a public asset—foremost as a source of clean water for the cities below. The state's action sparing uncut acreage to be "forever kept as wild forest land" became another milestone of forest conservation.

At the turn of the twentieth century, Gifford Pinchot introduced professional forestry to America with the goal of managing forests for the "greatest good for the greatest number." His vision for efficiency was an improvement over the cut-and-run pillaging that had marked the timber industry's march

SPRINGTIME FOREST **in Great Smoky Mountains National Park**

A thicket of maturing tuliptrees begins to leaf-out on a mountainside above the Oconaluftee River. Pure stands of one particular tree species such as this are often the result of a bumper year of seeds, or "mast," at the opportune time after the preceding forest had been cleared by fire, logging, insects, or disease.

CALIFORNIA BUCKEYES, **Arrastre Creek, California**

Bleached limbs of California buckeyes reach out over the parched foothills of the southern Sierra Nevada in autumn. The buckeyes go to seed quickly and drop their leaves in early summer in order to withstand intense heat and seasonal drought.

TULIPTREES with HICKORIES, Blue Ridge foothills, Virginia
Using a wide-angle lens to look straight up the trunk of a large tuliptree reveals the broadleaf's towering height and also the converging crowns of hickories, which all strive for maximum exposure to the sun's radiant energy.

Sunset light on LIVE OAKS, Cumberland Island National Seashore, Georgia
Colored by a hazy atmosphere, the setting southern sun beams into the junglelike thicket of saw palmettos and live oaks in springtime. Vines and mosses hang from every available surface. Spanish "moss" lives off air and water and uses the trees only for structural support.

across the continent, but it stopped far short of recognizing the aesthetic or ecological value of a native forest. At the same time, the idea of forest preservation was gaining ground. John Muir, who celebrated wild nature, wrote that forests "are useful not only as fountains of timber and irrigation rivers, but as fountains of life."

Prompted by Muir and others, public decisions to protect wild forests in national parks, state parks, and wilderness areas show that the beauty of forests became a key motivation to save natural wonders and wild places. In the 1930s, the hard-fought battle to set aside Olympic National Park in Washington marked another milestone—a forest of undeniably saleable trees was spared because of its intrinsic value.

Parklands were saved, but in the overall scheme of things, their acreage was small. And even while aged trees graced the calendars and the postcards that Americans selected as icons of their nation, the loss of old forests continued. Through the twentieth century the amount of uncut forest nationwide dwindled to 10 percent, then to 5 percent or less. A counter-movement, however, gradually gained strength. The fight to safeguard French Pete Valley in the Cascade Mountains of Oregon marked one of the clearest conflicts between logging and forest protection. Designation of wilderness there in 1978 boosted the movement to save uncut forests, and along with it, public acceptance of the notion that the beauty of a natural forest was worth saving.

In the 1980s an intensified movement, full of remarkable enthusiasm and determination, was based on increasing awareness of the scarcity of ancient forests and also of their irreplaceable ecological value. Support grew to spare the finest remaining giant trees in the Pacific Northwest, where only one out of every ten acres of original old-growth remained. In 1994

President Clinton's Northwest Forest Plan spared about two-thirds of the surviving uncut forests on federal land. This was followed by a decision under Forest Service Chief Mike Dombeck to ban new logging roads through most of the remaining untouched national forest. This action was backed by the largest outpouring of support ever documented for a decision regarding natural resources—1.2 million letters. Likewise, interest in protecting native forests spread throughout the country. Hundreds of organizations and thousands of people have become engaged in the fate of woodlands everywhere, from the permafrost edge of the Arctic to the darkened swamps of Louisiana. The image of wild, uncut trees has gained new cachet—American society has in large part come to see forests as valuable and beautiful. The stage is now set to treat this landscape differently than we have in the past, though the challenges in doing this—as we will see in chapter five—remain formidable.

TODAY, TREES ARE COMMON all around us, yet when I see them, and really notice them with open eyes and an open mind, they stir my spirit like few other things can. Sometimes I go out even when I can barely see the trees or forest at all. Long after sunset I've walked through the woods in darkness and been thrilled by everything around me: mysterious sounds coming from all sides; warm and cool currents of air as I crossed undulating ground; and the feel of organic soil underfoot, mixed with rocks and roots. In the pale light of the stars, or the moon, I've been awed by the black silhouettes of pines and oaks looming over me, all backed by a haunting depth of forest I could only imagine.

Nighttime walks in the woods are fascinating, but these adventures always leave me longing to know what is hidden. One brief hour in darkness makes me grateful for the gift of vision when the light returns in the morning and I can go out again and see—and really notice—the exquisite wild world of trees and forests.

PONDEROSA PINES, **Calaveras Big Trees State Park, California**
Silhouetted by moonlight, pines reach to great heights over a cone-shaped incense cedar and an intricate forest hidden by darkness until daybreak.

CHAPTER TWO

THE LIFE OF A TREE

FOR A FULL WEEK I walked through the woods of the Great Smoky Mountains. The fresh leaves and sweet blossoms of May enticed me onward to new views at every turn, and they also drew me to linger in the soft sunlight of spring. I stopped often, dropped my pack, and detoured where special sights caught my eye: century-old tuliptrees, the late-season unfurling of sycamore leaves, and the largest yellow buckeye I had ever seen.

I walked because I wanted to see the forests of the Smokies, but I had also come to see one particular tree, and when I found it, I planned to pay my deepest respects.

On my sixth day out, early in the evening, I knew I was getting close. The largest of all eastern hemlocks lay somewhere up ahead.

I had abandoned the trail, and now I crawled through thickets of rhododendron, stone-stepped across freshets of runoff, scrambled up slopes to circumvent cliffs, and crisscrossed the narrow Appalachian hollow as I kept looking, looking for the big tree. Elsewhere across America, many of the "champion" trees—the stately giants thought to be the largest of their kind—are isolated in backyards, at the edges of farmed fields, or just a step or two from a street. One of the largest eastern white pines, for example, was a breathtaking tree but stood two feet from a paved road at Morrill, Maine. Two feet! Taking its picture, I almost got run over! Here in the Smokies, I had no such problem. But in a forest thick with old trees, could I find the one hemlock that I had come so far to see?

Deep in mountain country, a thunderstorm of air-shattering severity had just passed, leaving me grateful that my search lay within a valley and not at the top of a peak rising up from lightening-prone ridgelines. My raincoat and pants had shed most of the deluge, but the potency of the storm left me damp in the late afternoon hour. Darkness, I knew, would come early in the narrow wooded hollow. Time, as always, was precious. I needed to find the tree soon.

Sizeable hemlocks grew alongside the rocky stream bottom and on north-facing slopes rising from it. Searching for a tree said to lean out over the creek, I continued through the temperate jungle of undergrowth, occasionally enjoying room-sized reprieves of openness beneath the impressive crowns of beech trees. And then, just ahead of me, I saw it.

The greatest of its tribe rose 165 feet—twice the height of many mature eastern hemlocks—with a diameter of about four feet where I reached out to touch it. Breezes ruffled its crown, but the massive base of the tree was so monumentally anchored in dirt and rock that I couldn't imagine it ever budging or changing. It was part of the landscape. Yet it was alive. Algae greened the grooved bark, as they had for several hundred years. Far up the clean canted bole, the first limb elbowed outward for light, and beyond it other branches textured the sky with the tiniest needles in the world of American conifers.

Savoring the moment, I sat in front of the tree, thinking about all the time it had lived. I speculated about the changes—seedling to sapling to giant—the tree had been through. Its life could read like a textbook on evolutionary success: The seed had been perfectly formed, it ripened at the critical time, fell propitiously from the crown or was harvested by a red squirrel, ended up in just the right spot for receptive soil and adequate moisture, then grew in its well-watered, wind-sheltered site. The great tree's ascendance was also an act of fortuitous chance against enormous odds. Out of millions of seeds from the now forgotten but no doubt impressive parent, this one took hold. It escaped browsing by deer and white-footed mice. Its tender young bark was passed over by roaming porcupines. It grew for hundreds of years, ultimately becoming the tallest known eastern hemlock in the world.

I thought about how triumphant this particular tree had been, reaching for light, producing new cones of its own, rooting itself firmly in the wild wooded earth. In the aftermath of the recent thunderstorm, an aroma of vitality wafted from rain-soaked surfaces of blossoms, new growth, and venerable rot all around me. Inhaling the fertile air deeply, I now stood and put both my hands on the tree, trying to see beyond what was clearly evident—trying to imagine the indomitable force of life inside the bark.

The tallest HEMLOCK, Great Smoky Mountains National Park
The largest known eastern hemlock stands tall in its "cove hardwood" community—an exceptionally diverse forest association where several dozen species of trees might appear in the canopy overhead. The soft light of this misty evening follows an afternoon thunderstorm that soaked the woods with rainfall.

Roots of a SUGAR MAPLE, Upper Peninsula, Michigan
A mature hardwood's web of roots can be seen here on this recently upended maple. Half the mass of some trees lies underground, where roots take in water, minerals, and nutrients essential to life. Valley oaks send roots down sixty feet deep; scrub oaks only three feet tall sometimes have roots twenty-five feet long in order to tap groundwater.

This particular hemlock had truly excelled, but every tree has the ability to astonish in its own way. And each tree species—some 679 to 865 of them in the United States depending on how subspecies are defined—is unique and extraordinary. As I sought out special trees such as the great hemlock, and as I photographed a variety of trees all across our country, I grew more and more interested in how they become what they are. I became more curious about how they do what they do.

Trees evolved from simpler plants by developing new abilities to store energy in seeds for germination when the time is right, reach high for sunlight, anchor themselves in the ground, catch and conserve precious water, and to fend off pests. Oaks five feet in diameter come from bite-size acorns. Redwood seeds might be mistaken for a spec of dirt, yet they grow into the tallest trees on earth. Sycamore or cottonwood seeds are almost invisible without a magnifying glass, but when the seeds ripen all together, they make summertime snowstorms as they float through the sky on wispy white plumes that seem lighter than air.

The seeds of a Coulter pine—along with many other pine species—lie deeply nested in the prickly hard encasement of cones that fall to the ground with a thud and remain there, sometimes for decades, until fire sweeps across the land. Then the heat of the flames opens the cones, the seeds pop out unharmed even after fifty years of waiting, and seedlings spring to life in the exposed soil. Many pines need fire, not only to open the cones, but also because the tiny seeds lack substantial stores of food and must root their way immediately into bare mineral soil lacking a shield of organic mulch.

DOWNY SERVICEBERRY, Swift River near Conway, New Hampshire

Flowers of the serviceberry are among the first to brighten the eastern forests in spring. Delicious purple seed-bearing fruits follow but are quickly plucked by robins, cardinals, and bluebirds.

BIGLEAF MAPLE above the Middle Fork Stanislaus River, California
Energy-packed maple buds are ready to burst with new leaves as springtime arrives at middle elevations of the Sierra Nevada.

EASTERN WHITE PINE CONES, Cascade River, Minnesota
Cones accumulate on the ground beneath a robust white pine in the North Woods. Nutty seeds of the white pine fall before thousands of cones drop from the branches, but many other species of pines produce cones that remain closed until fire opens them and releases the seeds for germination in freshly charred soil.

Using nothing but air, water, and a few trace minerals, trees make their own food. This is the purpose of leaves, and the food production process is called photosynthesis.

Microscopically embedded in each leaf, chlorophyll reacts with sunlight, and also with water and minerals brought up from the roots, and it converts them into glucose, or sugar. Along the way, carbon dioxide is pulled from the atmosphere and converted to solid carbon, which accounts for half (or more) of the tree's wood and solid substance. To add a pound of wood, an average tree "inhales" and retains one and one-half pounds of carbon dioxide through minute pores called stomata in the bottoms of the leaves. Thus, improbable as it may seem, trees are principally made of air. This discovery was gleaned four hundred years ago by J. B. van Helmont, a Flemish chemist who planted a tree in a tub and later determined that the tree gained 164 pounds but the weight of the soil was decreased by only two ounces—which is about as close as one can come to making something out of nothing. A large tree can sequester twenty-five to fifty pounds of carbon per year by taking it out of the air and converting it into wood.

Trees absorb carbon dioxide and expire oxygen. Having a reciprocal respiratory cycle, people expire carbon dioxide and breathe in about a pound of oxygen per day. This element, however, did not exist in the earth's original atmosphere. Oxygen first started to accumulate through photosynthesis by single-celled cyanobacteria, then by algae, and eventually—in a big way—by trees. Releasing oxygen, all these organisms revolutionized life on earth by creating breathable air. The amount of oxygen we each inhale daily is provided by one-twelfth of an acre of forest, which we might be wise to regard the same way a deep-sea diver thinks about the oxygen tank on his back.

Broadleaf trees are mostly deciduous, which means they drop their leaves each fall (most broadleaf, deciduous trees are also called "hardwoods," in contrast to conifers, which typically have softer wood). But a few broadleafs—such as magnolias and live oaks—keep their leaves all winter. A large oak might have seven hundred thousand leaves. Conifers—named because their seeds are produced in cones—have needles, which generally stay on throughout the winter, though larch trees shed their needles to cope with extreme cold in the far north, and baldcypresses in the South shed their needles as well. A large Douglas-fir has

MOUNTAIN ASH, Mount Pisgah, North Carolina
The mountain ash produces the most brilliant fruit of all American trees. This plentiful seed crop has ripened in early October as the leaves begin to fall, and will persist through winter and provide food for grosbeaks, cedar waxwings, and grouse.

sixty-five million needles. Conifers do well in regions with a dry summer climate, such as the mountains of California and the West, because needles lose less water to the atmosphere than do leaves. Furthermore, ponderosa and Jeffrey pines can take water in when nighttime dew condenses on their needles. These thirsty pines absorb the moisture and send it down to the roots, reversing the usual direction of water's flow. Conifers also excel during shorter summers of the North by not having to put energy into new leaf production each spring. Pines, likewise, populate the Southeast, where a combination of summer droughts, fast-drying sandy soil, and frequency of fires all favor needles and cones over leaves and fruits.

Deciduous trees drop their leaves in order to withstand low temperatures and to save energy, water, and food during winter. Taking cues from both shortening daylight and plummeting temperatures in the fall, they produce a corky "abscission" layer of cells between their leaf stems and twigs. This stops the flow of water to the leaves, which halts the production of chlorophyll. Throughout the summer chlorophyll absorbs the red and blue components of sunlight but not the green, which is reflected back and becomes visible. Thus, chlorophyll is what makes much of the outdoor world green. Without it—as autumn advances—other colors inherent in the leaf begin to appear: yellow, orange, and red. Each tree has a different suite of chemical pigments, so

MOUNTAIN ASH and THIMBLEBERRY in the Rogue River Gorge, Oregon
Green compound leaves of the mountain ash reach out for sunlight within the deep, shaded forest of the Rogue River Gorge.

FLOWERING DOGWOOD at **Tamarack Bog, Indiana**
In autumn, shortening days and colder temperatures trigger deciduous trees to stop the flow of water and nutrients to the leaves. Chlorophyll production is halted, and the leaves begin to turn red, yellow, and orange. Seeds for the dogwood's next generation are packed in festive red berries.

each shows different colors, with spectacular results overall in a deciduous forest in October.

The leaves produce the food, which is promptly fed via veins to the trunk and branches so that they can grow and reach for more light, and thereby produce more food. The cambium of trees, so thin that a microscope is needed to see it, is the critical zone where growth occurs—a layer of cells running the length and circumference of the trunk and its branches and lying just inside the bark, like a cylinder. On the outside veneer of this cylinder, a layer of cells called the phloem carries the downward flow of foodstuffs from the leaves to the rest of the tree, including its roots. On the interior of the cambium, the sapwood (also called xylem) carries water and minerals up from the roots to the ends of the twigs and to the leaves.

The tree and its branches get longer, not by pushing up from their bases as grasses do, but by extending the tips of the twigs. Likewise, the tree gets fatter by adding a thin layer of new cells to the outside of the sapwood. Each summer another concentric layer of wood is added, resulting in the distinct annual growth rings that can be counted when the trunk is cut.

While new rings accumulate at the outside circumference of the trunk, the cellular chambers of the previous layers of wood on the inside of the tree become clogged. With vital fluids blocked there, the center of the tree dies and darkens into hard wood called lignin. This is the heartwood—the rigid, structural core that makes trees "trees" and enables them to be tall. The most light—and thereby the most photosynthesis—rewards the trees that rise the highest.

The tallest trees, coast redwoods, can reach 300 feet and more. The tallest redwood that is known at this time, named "Hyperion," is 378 feet—a forty-story skyscraper. Douglas-firs can reach 300 feet, and sugar pines—largest in their genus—can reach 250.

Largest in mass, one giant sequoia in California sports a diameter of thirty-six feet—the width of a sizeable house. Western hemlocks, Sitka spruces, grand firs, and western redcedars likewise become enormous.

With severe windstorms always possible and a host of genetic traits at play, eastern trees don't grow as large as the western giants, but in the scale of their surrounding forests, big trees in the East are also impressive. Before the original cutting of the forest, white pines reached 240 feet according to Donald Culross Peattie. The tallest today is 207 feet, and most are much shorter. Topping the charts for mass among eastern trees, one sycamore in Kentucky bellies-out with a diameter of six feet. Tulip poplars up to five feet across crown a number of eastern stands. Live oaks, along with red and white oaks, American elms, and eastern cottonwoods, can have diameters of three feet and more.

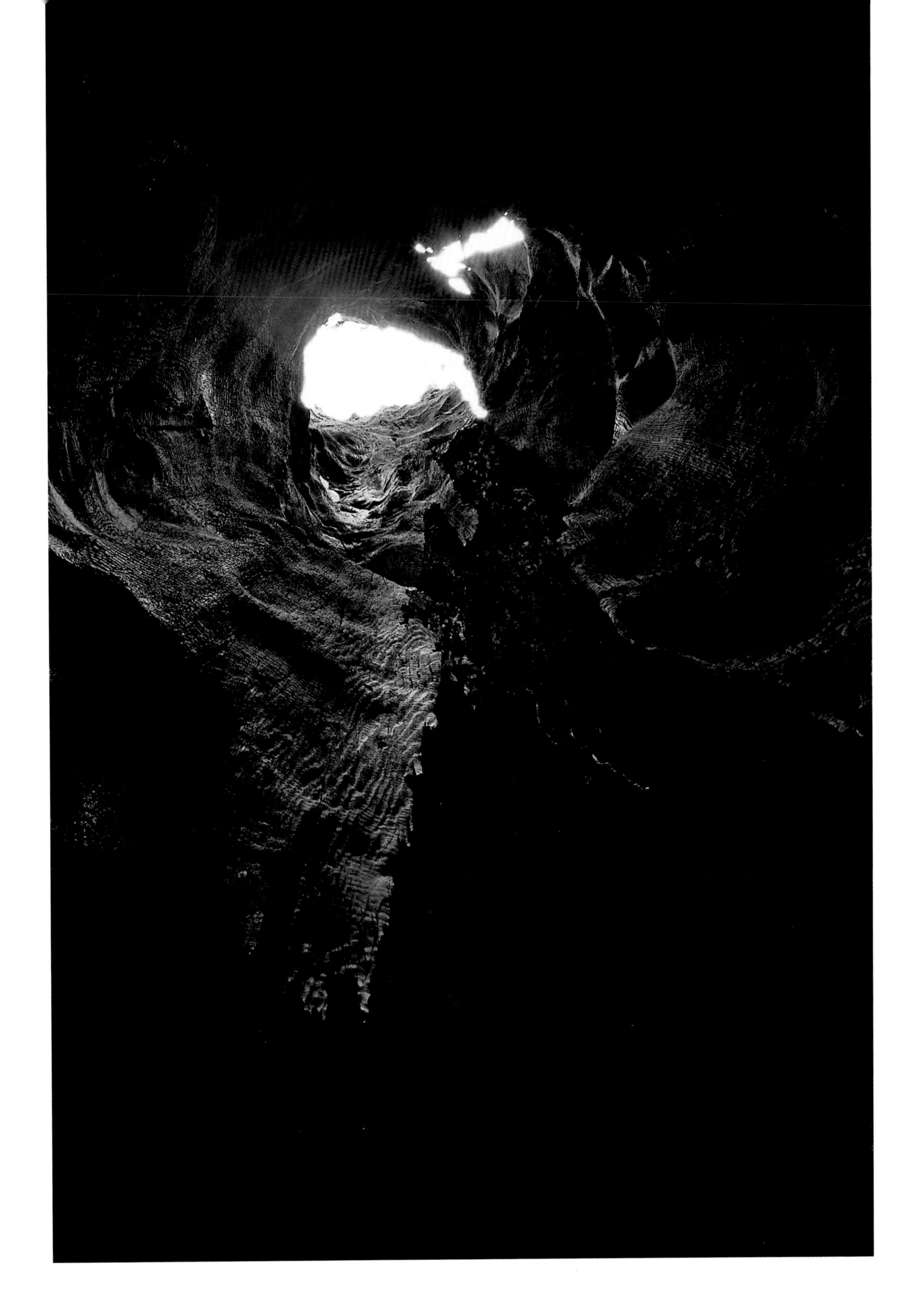

BLACK COTTONWOOD, **Willamette Mission State Park, Oregon**
Considered the largest of its species, this black cottonwood rises 158 feet. Massive cottonwoods were once found along many rivers, but the following generations were often thwarted by uncontrolled grazing, diversions of water, and flood-control dams. The dams eliminate high water and its accompanying silt deposits, which are necessary for the germination of cottonwood seeds. Here, compound leaves of a black walnut tree wave in the foreground.

Standing REDWOOD BOLE, **southern Oregon**
From inside the trunk of a giant, hollowed-out redwood, this view shows the remains of a great tree that was repeatedly burned in the Winchuck Grove—one of the northernmost redwood stands.

JEFFREY PINE BARK, **Lake Tahoe, California**
As trees add annual rings of sapwood, the bark expands by cracking, flaking, or peeling while corky new protective tissue forms underneath. Jeffrey, ponderosa, and other pines crack with ridges, plates, and scaly flakes that expand outward and guard the tree against pests, weather, and fire.

The shape of a tree is determined by its quest for light and also by deep genetic codes. Most trees fill out in spreading crowns if they have space around them; this maximizes the chance for leaves to intercept sunlight and photosynthesize. If crowded together, as they usually are in a forest, trees become taller and thinner because the sunlight is found in only one direction—up. Beyond these generalities, each species is shaped differently. Oaks have rounded crowns, while firs are pointed. Longleaf pines have flattened tops, which take advantage of light that appears directly overhead at southern latitudes. Sugar pines have long upturned branches. Elms crown out like an umbrella. Each shape serves an effective strategy for survival.

Along this line, each species also responds to snow in its own way. Subalpine firs are pointed like obelisks so that they shed snow readily. Mountain hemlocks have supple branches; they finesse the winter storms by bending to drop each new load of snow. Junipers bulk up in thick, stiff, muscular branches that bear the weight of heavy snowpacks by brute force.

The bark protects the inner organism from desiccation, evaporation, insects, disease-bearing microbes, and sunlight. As the tree gets larger, the bark must expand. It does this by cracking and producing a new corklike layer underneath, while the old, dead bark is pushed outward as a dispensable shield on the vanguard of contact with the rest of the world.

WESTERN HEMLOCKS **in the Elk River watershed, Oregon**
Well suited to the hazards of mountain snowstorms, which can come even in late spring, hemlock limbs bend downward under the weight of new snow until they drop the heavy load to the ground. Unharmed, the limbs spring back into place, where they are able to resume catching sunlight and photosynthesizing. Each species of tree has its own adaptations to snow and to other climatic conditions wherever they live.

The bark of each species cracks and expands differently, and the resulting patterns are another way to tell one type of tree from another. Pine bark cracks in plates; geometric designs that fit together like pieces of a puzzle are diagnostic of ponderosa, Jeffrey, red, and longleaf pines. The bark of a Douglas-fir has thick ridges with deep furrows in between—a bulky, fireproof coat. Dogwoods have crazed bark with finely textured crack lines. Alligator juniper, found not in swamps of the Southeast but in semi-arid Arizona, has bark that resembles alligator skin. Redwood bark appears in long fibrous lines, almost like fur. Atypically, beeches have bark that continues to grow as the tree does, and so remains smooth and uniquely beautiful. Birches also do this to a degree, though their papery bark can be peeled off in layers smooth enough for writing on and large enough for sheeting canoes.

In areas that frequently burn, fireproof bark is an asset if not a necessity. The giant sequoias produce a foot-thick skin that lacks resin, and therefore carries little flame. This and other species also have tannins in the bark, which repel insects. Some birds take dust baths at the bases of these trees in order to pick up particles of the tannin-laden bark and thereby gain relief from pesky bugs.

All these adaptations and many more combine to make trees not only the tallest and largest, but also the oldest living organisms on earth. The Egyptian pyramids are old, but they are made of rock; bristlecone pines are just as old but have been *alive* the entire time. Located in isolated groves on high peaks in Nevada, Colorado, Utah, and southeastern California, bristlecones have lived for forty-eight hundred years and counting. One ironic reason for the bristlecones' longevity is that they occupy sparse sites, beyond the range of fire, pests, and competitors at eleven thousand feet, and on steep slopes receiving only eight inches of precipitation a year—most of it snow. Each growth ring is as thin as a human hair, if that. Similarly ancient, but with a lot of wood to show for it, giant sequoias can live three thousand years.

BRISTLECONE PINE, White Mountains, California
Bristlecones are the oldest trees and oldest organisms on earth, living up to 4,800 years. In spare soil at a high elevation, this tree survives even on a wind-eroded site in the Schulman Grove, east of Bishop. Some standing bristlecone snags have been dead for two thousand years.

After trees die, they continue to support life. In fact, dead trees typically house more life than live ones. Mosses, lichens, and molds cover the fallen trunks and create entire habitats for other plants and animals. Mushrooms, ferns, huckleberries, and whole new trees sprout from rotting bark. Mammals and birds occupy cavities of both standing and fallen dead trees. Insects by the millions and microbes by the billions decompose the wood and serve as food for a pyramid of larger creatures. A third of the dead wood is returned to soil by termites—bad players in our own houses but essential workers in the ecology of the forest. A large Douglas-fir will spend five hundred years rotting into the ground, all that time supporting a plethora of life. And after that, the tree's remains become soil that nourishes other plants and animals for all time. Trees really are immortal.

Back there in the heart of the Smoky Mountains, where I respectfully stood beside the greatest of all eastern hemlocks, I reflected on some of these far-ranging contributions that each tree makes to the world. As I stood with my hands on that hemlock, I also wondered about its fate. Will the great evergreen die of natural causes? In that remote Appalachian hollow, it was difficult to imagine anything *but* natural causes. And yet, I wondered.

In all their composite parts and in all their strategies for thriving, trees master the challenges of their local settings with intricate means that they've refined through the millennia. The details of each tree—whether in its seeds, leaves, bark, shape, roots, or autumn color—are not only beautiful but also practical, with the perfection of form matching function. Combined, the trees and all the life associated with them form a forest with webs of endless connections that serve the rest of life on earth.

BLACK WILLOWS, **Mississippi River, Arkansas**
Requiring a constant water supply, and also adapted to seasonal flooding with supple limbs that easily bend in swift current, black willows take root at the edges of rivers and on the lower limits of silty floodplains throughout their broad range across America.

CHAPTER THREE

THE NATURE OF THE FOREST

To reach one of the finest remaining uncut forests on the West Coast, Jim Rogers and I drove for twenty miles up the winding course of the Elk River in southern Oregon. Each curve took us deeper into the shaded recess of steep mountains darkened by evergreens, alders, and maples. Then, climbing out of the valley, we traveled for another hour on gravel roads, curving high to a mountain pass and eventually to a nondescript pullout thickened with brush. I grabbed my camera bag and slung my tripod over my shoulder, and we began to walk.

Rarely do I have a guide for these kinds of expeditions, but today Jim was leading the way. Otherwise, I would have had difficulty finding the big forest, unmarked on maps but lying somewhere up ahead. Furthermore, the big forest would probably not even be there if it weren't for Jim.

We soon crested a small hilltop that separated the road behind us from the deep woods to come, and then we worked our way down a mountainside packed with twenty-foot trees, barbed stems of salmonberries, and a lush undergrowth of ferns. Mushrooms had responded to the first storms of autumn, popping out of dampened ground and signaling the beginning of a new rainy season that would intermittently drench the spectacular chaos of this rugged landscape for eight months. For every fifty feet of elevation gained as we had driven up from sea level, annual precipitation increased a full inch owing to cooler temperatures. Where we now walked, a hundred inches might fall in a year. The southern reaches of the world's greatest temperate rainforest are the incredible result, and that is what we had come to see.

Jim had worked for the timber industry for several decades—much of that time as the chief forester who found and marked the trees that would be cut for a plywood mill nearby. He kept the sawyers supplied with logs for years, but not without some misgivings. Old trees were being cut at an unsustainable rate. Habitat for wildlife that needed undisturbed forests was being lost. Eventually Jim parted ways with the industry and set off on his own as a seasoned forester, field-trained wildlife expert, and fearless conservationist. Having cut his share of trees in these woods, Jim adopted a new mission to protect the finest that remained.

DOUGLAS-FIR, Copper Salmon Wilderness, Oregon
A centuries-old Douglas-fir has aged in the organic mulch of an undisturbed forest floor. A Port Orford cedar rises on the right.

RED PINES and CENTRAL HARDWOODS, **Pine Creek watershed, Pennsylvania**
These pines of the northeast and northcentral states grow amid a forest of richly diverse trees supporting life of many kinds. Red pines mix together with eastern white pines but also thrive on soils too rocky and infertile for those larger trees. Roots of red pines readily intertwine, enabling trees along streams to transfer water to their neighbors on drier sites.

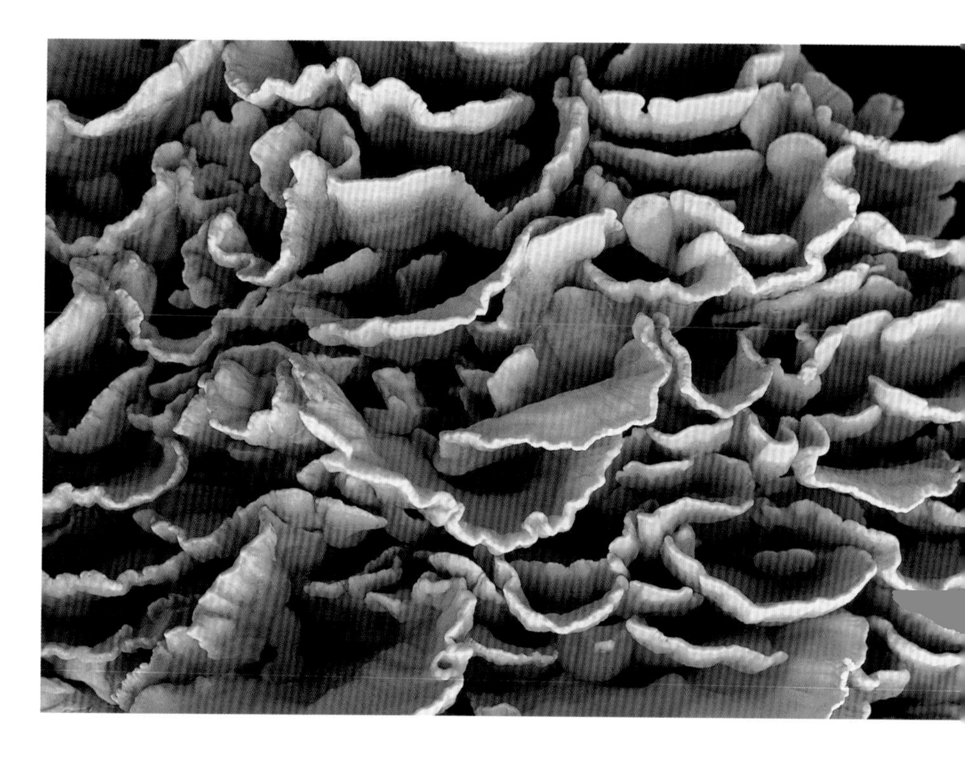

FUNGUS on a dead tree, Hoh River Valley, Olympic National Park, Washington
Fungi ripen in fruiting colonies on rotting wood and spread in thin strands that permeate the soil surrounding trees—provided that the soil is largely undisturbed. In a symbiotic relationship, the fungi help the trees, boosting their growth rates by 20 percent and more.

Jim walked with the measured pace of a sixty-four-year-old man who still spends three out of four days working outdoors, and he answered my questions about the makeup of nature here, and about his steadfast goal. He wants Congress to designate twelve thousand acres of trees as the Copper Salmon Wilderness, named for two mountains that define the headwaters of the Elk River. The softened summits and their steep, green slopes cup the upper basin like a great amphitheater. Here, an out-sized drama of creation has been playing nonstop for the ages. It's quite a show, and in the wilderness area, we will get to see this creation as it really is—untouched by people, or at least untouched by people with chainsaws and bulldozers. Only 5 percent of the great forests of the Oregon Coast Range remain uncut, and this was the finest unprotected piece remaining.

In awhile we struck out off-trail, dipping sharply downhill to where the trees grew large, the trunks darkly shaded and furred in moss as thick as a bear's fur in winter. In another ten minutes the slope flattened somewhat, and Jim paused, and stood quietly where his grizzled beard, wool cap, and briar-worn jacket seemed to match the age, the shagginess, and the rough-cut determination of life all around him. I could see that we had arrived at the edge of the great grove, dark, silent, and hidden, as if it lay recessed in the forested wilds of a fable.

Enduring Douglas-firs grew six to ten feet in diameter and towered up to the sky—the whole way, as near as I could tell from my vantage point beneath the thick crowning foliage. Somewhat smaller western hemlocks also rose from the spongy, porous, organic mulch underfoot. This seemed to be half air and half mossy rotting wood, with only a trace of mineral soil down there somewhere. Now and then my boots would break through and become momentarily stuck among roots and shards of cellulose in all phases of buggy decomposition. An entire ecosystem of untold complexity lay beneath each footstep.

Catching my eye most, the rare Port Orford cedar lives only along the southern Oregon coast and nearby mountains. This conifer is so favored as decorative wood that its logs—so much like columns in a cathedral when alive—bring five times the money of pricey, fine-grained redwood when cut, trucked, stacked, and shipped overseas to Japan, where the similar hinoki cypress has been driven to the brink of extinction.

For clinching evidence of the biological perils of globalism, one need look no further than this extremely localized tree. While most old boles of magnificent stature have been shipped to Japan, most of the young trees are now being killed by a fungus inadvertently introduced into America from ornamental nursery stock imported from Asia. The fungus is spread by water, including mud temporarily lodged in the tires of cars and—more important on the spaghetti-network of dirt roads built to extract timber—in the fat-tire treads of logging trucks. As a result, anywhere roads pass uphill from a tree, the cedars have been killed, with the rare exception of individuals that resist the disease through a fortunate quirk of genetics. For now, isolated within this proposed wilderness area, the giant cedars appear to be safe, but only if the roads can be kept out.

The cedar's welfare alone would be good enough reason to designate this national forest tract—owned by all Americans—as wilderness. And if that weren't enough, the scarcity of remaining old-growth timber would be adequate rationale to persuade me. But Jim's main motivation was to protect the Elk River. "If these steep mountainsides were logged," he explained, "silt would run into the river down below and cover the gravel with sediment and ruin the spawning beds that the salmon and steelhead need. The runoff would come faster, and crest higher, then drop sooner, and dry up in summer. All that would play havoc with the fish as they swim up river and try to spawn." By many accounts, the Elk is one of the finest salmon streams of its size on the West Coast south of Canada. Now I learn that its fishery depends on the trees that grace its banks and its mountainsides, on the branches that green its headwaters and tributary basins, and on the roots, needles, cones, seeds, and interwoven community of life made possible only by these woods.

Rivers need forests. Fish need trees.

Climbing with effort over fallen firs that take me six feet off the ground, picking my way across ravines packed with rotting wood as though gravity has crammed stick after stick into every depression in the ground for ages, and bulling my way through minor thickets of evergreen huckleberries laced with the crooked and tangled stems of rhododendrons, I wandered farther into the grove of giant trees. With each step I took, the place seemed more enchanted.

The wind, which had blown forcefully on the ridge above, barely whispered down here, deep under the canopy where for centuries silence has prevailed, except for the occasional thunderous falling of a tree. Billions of branches, twigs, and needles block out the direct rays of the sun, leaving just a few errant beams to backlight the translucent foliage of bigleaf maples. Their sharply toothed leaves are big for a reason; they need every square inch they can muster to catch the muted residue of sunlight filtering through the evergreens.

ENGELMANN SPRUCES and LODGEPOLE PINES in winter, Galena Pass, Idaho

Spruces and lodgepole pines cover mountain flanks and accommodate heavy snowfalls in the mountains of central Idaho. Conifers do well in wintry regions because they can withstand heavy snow, and they don't need to produce new leaves during the brief growing season.

Even at a glance it was amply evident that the forest's many life-forms are connected—not just in function, not just in ecology with its myriad linkages between living and dead organisms and with diagrammatic relationships between producers and consumers—but literally connected: physically joined. The roots of everything are seamlessly intertwined underfoot like some great orgy of touch—a degree of mingling that simply isn't acceptable or possible above ground. The mosses overhead completely cover the branches as if dressing the whole woods for an expedition to the arctic. The trees rise high into the sky while penetrating deep into the soil, linking air and earth as nothing else can do. Fog accumulates on needles and twigs—on all the outside surfaces of the trees—and once there's enough, it drips down on the ground. Immediately, it is sponged up by the duff, where root hairs—billions and billions of them—lie in thirsty wait. The water is sucked up again through capillary action—this time on the *inside* of the trees—all the way back to the treetops, two hundred feet up and even higher, which is a long way to lift something as heavy as water. In this way, the forests drink the fog.

Hemlocks lean against firs. Wild cucumbers grip tenaciously on limbs and dangle from them like vines in the tropics. Lichens color tree trunks with articulated splotches of free-form art. Licorice ferns decorate bonsai gardens on top of large limbs even eighty feet above the ground. Along with many lichens, lycopods, and mosses, these are epiphytes—plants that anchor themselves on trees but draw their sustenance entirely from air and rainfall.

I sensed the connections to other animate life—to whole throngs of it. A squirrel chattered at me territorially while it harvested cones. A varied thrush fluttered secretively, seeking dinner amid the brush. Though a bear had left no tracks on the resilient carpet of plantlife, I saw its black, berry-filled scat—unmistakable evidence of recent passing. Now, from Jim, I learned that the forest's connections extend to the river in the valley below, to the fish swimming and spawning there, and even far downstream to the estuaries and ocean where the fish spend several years of adult life. Leaping to the next conceptual step, I imagined molecules of organic matter and water being linked together as one seamless artery from here to the sea, and I realized that life flows back and forth through that lifeline as long as the medium is not severed by a road, a dam, or any

BIGLEAF MAPLE with mosses and lichens, Coast Range, southern Oregon
Mosses and lichens drape the limbs of bigleaf maples and can account for four times as much weight as the leaves of the tree. Beneficial and often essential to their arboreal hosts, these primitive plants help the tree to collect water, absorb nutrients, and fend off insect pests. White alders and tanoaks fill the background.

MULE DEER near Hurricane Ridge, Olympic Mountains, Washington
At the edge of a mountain hemlock forest, a mule deer browses on a groundcover of forbs and grasses. The deer depend on thick forests for shelter in winter.

other dead zone, which might be as thin as one swipe of a bulldozer's blade.

In this rare surviving wilderness, it could not have been more apparent that a forest is emphatically more than just a collection of trees. It's more than a legion of trunks anchored in dirt as if each bole were just a big toothpick stuck in sand for support. Rather, the forest is a vast system of soil, minerals, air, water, and all manner of creatures in this intricately evolved, highly mature, and stunningly verdant garden of life.

THE FORESTS OF AMERICA house thousands of kinds of creatures, microbes to moose. Forests occupy about half the land area of America (grasslands, deserts, high country, tundra, pavement, and buildings account for the other half), and among all our landscapes, the forested lands are the richest in species and greatest in biomass. Their web of organic extravagance extends from multimillions of microbes under each square foot of earth up through the rootmasses and groundcovers and shrubs and saplings and tree trunks, all the way up to towering crowns with leaves and needles that dress these veritable skyscrapers of the natural world.

In healthy forests, warblers and dozens of other songbird species occupy the tops of deciduous trees. We hardly ever see them because they dart and perch out of sight amid the leaves, but they can be heard singing their hearts out in springtime, an orchestra bursting with proud announcements of passion: They want to mate. Lower down on those trees, dark cavities aren't just holes in rotten old trunks but homes to chickadees, nuthatches, woodpeckers, sapsuckers, barred owls, and mergansers, and also to raccoons and fishers. As the largest member of the weasel family, fishers are sleek, otter-shaped predators of awesome capabilities, so elusive almost nobody ever sees them.

Many birds and animals simply find holes in trees and claim them. But some of these homes are made to order. The red-cockaded woodpecker, for example, spends two years excavating a cavity before calling its digs complete. Owing to the scarcity of longleaf pines big enough for this kind of nest in today's South, the colorful, splendidly architectural woodpecker is threatened.

In a classic case of interdependence, several species of pines, including the whitebark, limber, and foxtail, are so dependent on the lives of the Clark's nutcracker and a few other members of

ALDER LEAVES and soil erosion, lower Umpqua River, Oregon
These alder leaves had fallen to the ground in an area recently scalped bare by the clearcutting of timber. Heavy rains followed, causing erosion wherever raindrops landed on exposed soil. This picture shows that even a single layer of alder leaves offered enough protection to avoid major soil loss; after the storm, the leaves stood on pedestals of uneroded dirt one inch high. To create an inch of new soil, natural processes require up to five hundred years.

the jay family that they are called the "bird pines." The wingless seeds of the trees remain tightly ensconced in their cones and drop to the ground with little apparent promise of germinating up in snow-laden high country where fires seldom burn. But the nutcrackers forcibly extract the seeds and pack up to eighty at a time into a specially designed pouch within their mouths. Then they bury the seeds for eating later. With eyes far bigger than its stomach, a single nutcracker stores up to ninety thousand seeds a year. Thousands are not retrieved, and therefore sprout into whole new forests that will feed more birds as well as red squirrels and other animals. Even nine-hundred-pound grizzly bears take advantage of the crop by pawing up the food caches of squirrels and gouging delicious mouthfuls of buried nuts in order to fatten up before turning in for hibernation each fall.

Underneath protective canopies of trees—especially evergreens such as hemlocks—deer find shelter during even the harshest winter storms. These lean ungulates eat almost any vegetation in the woods—they love poison oak, for example. When deer numbers are too plentiful, owing to the lack of top predators such as wolves and to inadequate hunting by people in the wolves' absence, the deer's feeding zone can be recognized by a "browse line" where greenery is totally absent below the five-foot level of limbs. (The stress that this imbalance places on plantlife, including rare species, can be extreme.)

Moose browse on the twigs, buds, and other nutritious morsels of the riverfront woods. In the lean months of winter, turkeys scratch for food in places where evergreens intercept snowfall and shelter the ground underneath.

In the Rocky Mountains of Colorado, red-naped sapsuckers—brilliant with crimson heads and throats—drill "wells" in the stems of willow trees to suck up the sugary sap. Some forty other birds, mammals, and insects are drawn to the same sap wells for food. The sapsuckers also excavate nesting holes in aspen trees, selecting those that are presoftened by a native heartwood fungus. Even when the previous year's nesting sites are available, the birds create new holes each spring. Seven different kinds of birds readily occupy the old vacant sites. The trees and the sapsuckers, in tandem, are critical to all these other species, and additional dependencies ripple out from there.

In the Northwest, trees and their rotting remains are home to myriad fungi, which include truffles as underground fruiting bodies. Mouselike voles live on the nutritious truffles. Vole droppings include truffle spores, and in this way the voles spread the fungi, which are beneficial to the trees. Meanwhile, spotted

BOX ELDER along the Clinch River, Virginia
Forests along riverfronts stabilize the banks against erosion, shade the water and keep it cool for native fish, filter silt and pollution that seep toward the rivers from farmed fields, and provide the most productive of all wildlife habitat—the streamside belt of trees called a riparian zone.

owls, which live only in large trees, eat the voles, and thus keep the numbers of these little rodents in check so they don't overplay their role in the greater scheme of things. Tree-fungi-truffle-vole-owl-tree—this is just one among many circles of life in the forest. Take away one member—for example, the owls, which happen to be imperiled because they need large tracts of ancient forest—and the rest are in danger of destabilization and even extinction in some cases.

At the Copper Salmon Wilderness, Jim Rogers explained how the old-growth forest keeps streams clean and healthy enough to support annual runs of salmon, which many of us eat. And the forest-to-fish association extends to other life as well. Biologists found that twenty-one species of wildlife feed directly on salmon of the Soleduck River in Olympic National Park. Black and brown bears fish for salmon; one researcher found that each bear along a healthy stream in British Columbia caught up to five hundred fish a year. Because the bears abandon partially eaten meals in the woods, and because the digested remains of the fish are likewise deposited as scat by the bears, virtually all the salmon that are caught by bears end up fertilizing the forests where the bears live. Tree-stream-salmon-bear-tree—this is another circle of woodland connections, though it is broken when the salmon populations crash because of dams, pollution, overfishing, or damage to spawning streams in the wake of careless logging.

Salmon and bears can really catch our attention, but the connections between trees and other forest life are often unseen, unheard, unrealized. Half the biomass of some trees lies hidden underground as roots, and these live in association with staggering quantities of invisible life. One square yard of forest soil can contain 2,000 individual earthworms, 40,000 insects, 120,000 mites, 120 million nematodes, and bacteria in unfathomable numbers. These creatures exhale carbon dioxide essential to tree roots. This relationship between unequal yet dependent partners—carried out underground on a massive scale in utter darkness—has all the intimacy of mouth-to-mouth resuscitation.

If we look carefully at an Appalachian forest, we can find a riot of forest-floor activity in salamanders. Up to 320 per acre scurry through leaf litter and account for more biomass than any other vertebrate in the woods, including deer. A hundred different bird species alone use California oak woodlands, as do sixty kinds of mammals and five thousand varieties of insects. Some of these are eaten by other birds that don't even go into the woods, and some of these insects leave the woods for parts of their lives and keep commercial crops extant by pollinating them.

One square foot of soil in an old northwestern forest can house 250 different species of invertebrates, all of which have a role to play in the health of the woods. This—and not just dirt weathering from rock—is what makes forest soil fertile and productive for all life, including the trees we cut for the homes we build.

Seldom noticed, a hundred species of lichen live in the canopy of a northwestern forest. Their weight on a bigleaf maple can exceed four times that of the tree's own leaves. When it rains, these basic building blocks of the forest community trap moisture and retard its runoff, but eventually the water drips down from the lichens and feeds the roots of the trees. Lichens, despite their size, are a primary food source for animals as large as the endangered woodland caribou in northern Idaho. In forests throughout the northern and middle latitudes, lichens fall to the ground when ice-laden branches break. Delivered to wildlife's doorstep when other foods are buried in snow, the lichens serve as emergency forage for deer and other animals that converge under the canopy as if it were a big tent thrown up for shelter in a storm. Furthermore, while living in their canopy-perches, the lichens take nitrogen out of the atmosphere and store it in their tissues, and when dead, they fall to the ground and fertilize the soil with this valuable element—essential to other life.

Multitudes of plants and animals depend on the trees, and it also works the other way—the trees depend on other plants, mammals, birds, and even fish, as we saw with the rotting carcasses of salmon. Some of those fish measure three feet long, but in many cases the smaller the organism, the greater

REDWOODS rising into the fog, northern California
Trees shade, cool, and shelter the earth. They keep it moist, and they even convert fog into usable precipitation. These redwoods push their crowns high into the sky, where plentiful needles intercept the moisture-laden air. This liquefies on the surfaces of the needles, accumulates, and eventually drips to the ground, nourishing the tree and all of its associated life. Fog drip can account for ten or more inches of precipitation a year and up to 35 percent of a forest's annual water supply in the Northwest.

the effect. Mycorrhizae fungi, for example, are not just musty old parasites webbed into rotting soil, but rather organisms that beneficially wrap themselves around tree roots and help in collecting water and in taking up phosphorus, nutrients, and minerals. Firs, cedars, spruces, and all the choice trees for lumber depend on these fungi hitching themselves to tiny root hairs, as do the deciduous beeches, oaks, walnuts, and others. Mycologists have found that fungi attached to tree roots can put a tree in contact with one thousand times more soil than can the roots alone. The aid of unseen fungi bolsters the growth rate of pines by 20 percent.

Seemingly prescient, trees extract nitrogen from their leaves before they allow them to drop in the autumn. They convey this nutritious chemical-food down to the roots for use in the lean months to come. Along this line, many trees nearing death will sacrifice available energy to produce a bumper crop of cones or seeds, effectively sacrificing time-limited resources to the next generation.

Even more amazing, a Douglas-fir nearing death will similarly send its remaining chemical assets down its trunk and out its roots to the mycorrhizae fungi that intertwine among myriad other roots of the forest. The communal fungi then transfer these essential products to neighboring trees—many of which may be direct offspring of the Douglas-fir that's about to die. The trees appear to have mastered the art of inheritance in ways scarcely imaginable to us, and one might be tempted to use the word "altruism."

All the fungi, lichens, microbes, and other invisibles—present only if the soil is healthy—are essential in order for trees to live. They're needed for the entire forest ecosystem to thrive. And when it does, the trees and related vegetation—including berries, mushrooms, nuts, seeds, twigs, buds, bark, and leaves—feed a menagerie of wildlife including herbivores such as squirrels and deer, carnivores such as martens and fishers, and omnivores such as bears, raccoons, and people. All of this is in jeopardy when logging or development damages soil through excavation, scarring, herbicide spraying, or compaction caused by simply driving heavy equipment across the ground.

When considering the connections among different forms of life in different kinds of woodlands, old-growth forests, such as Copper Salmon, are in a class by themselves. They are typified by trees one hundred or more years old and by a densely shaded canopy. However, small openings also exist owing to spot fires or to trees being uprooted by wind. These allow for sunny spaces where seedlings can germinate and prosper, resulting in a mix of tree sizes and species. Most old-growth forests have multi-layered canopies, dead trees in varying degrees of rot, standing snags with cavities where limbs have fallen or the wood has been fractured, and a plethora of shade-tolerant plants underneath. These are the classic big woods where one can walk quietly on soft paths and be awed by the greatness of life that has lived for centuries. Elsewhere, single large trees or small groves are attractive or important, but without the full suite of woodland species on a sizeable tract of land, isolated trees don't even come close to offering the biological and ecological qualities of a whole, intact, aged forest.

Old forests are needed by many species of wildlife, each depending on various traits of shade and shelter, diversity and specialization, complexity and interdependence within the woods. Most celebrated, the spotted owl requires old-growth for shelter, nesting sites, and food; 95 percent of the birds live in trees that are at least two hundred years old. Another "indicator species," the marbled murrelet spends most of its life on the ocean but nests and rears its young on the high, fat branches of old trees. The birds fish at sea but then fly their catch home to feed their chicks—sometimes winging a remarkable fifty miles just to get to the essential big tree where the family resides.

WHETHER AS OLD-GROWTH or regrowing trees, the workings of the forest ecosystem are not just critical to the plants and animals that live there, but to the health of the whole earth. Forests are backstage operatives, for example, in the hydrologic cycle. Woodlands everywhere serve as natural reservoirs that dwarf, by far, all the dammed-up reservoirs ever built on rivers.

DRIFTWOOD on the beach, Cape Blanco, Oregon
Some trees fall into rivers, drift with the current, and get stuck in logjams. The submerged or piled-up wood offers great benefits to the streams by providing habitat and a nutrient base for microscopic decomposers and insects at the bottom of the food chain. Eventually, some of the logs get washed to sea, where they might float great distances before being swept back to shore. Ultimately the driftwood creates new woody habitat for another whole community of life along the edge of ocean beaches.

TULIPTREES, SYCAMORES, and BEECHES, Rock Creek Park, Washington, D.C.

Even within some of our large urban areas, rich forests can be found, thanks to the establishment of public parks many years ago. However, new park acquisitions do not keep up with population growth. Here sycamores with white trunks rise behind stately tuliptrees and young beeches in full autumn color.

BASSWOODS and SILVER MAPLES, Nerstrand-Big Woods State Park, Minnesota

Forests are more than just trees. The mix of species, the collections of forbs, ferns, and shrubs in the understory, the presence of old trees with hollowed-out cavities where birds and animals can nest and live, and the intermittent supply of decomposing limbs on the ground are all important features of arboreal ecosystems.

An undisturbed forest floor in the Northwest can soak-up twelve inches of rainfall in an hour. Hydrologists have found that, through water storage in the root zones, mature woodlands in the East can reduce some flood levels by 75 percent.

Runoff from a healthy forest is generally clean, and the older the forest, the cleaner the water is likely to be. This is unlike the silt-laden flows from cutover land scarred with roads where runoff chews into the soil and washes it away. The forests' role in sustaining water quality serves people's needs directly and, for this reason alone, protection of forests is an economic issue of top importance. Because more than half of the nation's drinking water comes from runoff of forests, their protection is essential to public health. Facing the prospect of paying eight billion dollars or more to build treatment plants to make water drinkable, New York City in the 1990s opted to spend one billion dollars to safeguard the forested watersheds surrounding its reservoirs by acquiring development rights.

We know how important heating and cooling systems are to our houses, but it's the forests that help to regulate the temperature of the big home. Forests warm whole landscapes with shelter in winter, and they cool the land with shade in summer. Just a few trees can make a difference, especially in urban and suburban neighborhoods. Air conditioning costs in sweltering Atlanta, for example, can be decreased by 40 percent if a homeowner plants only three trees. The shaded sides of homes are often fifteen degrees cooler than the sunny sides. Because the chemical process of evaporation consumes heat, a forest's routine transpiration of water—taking it in liquid form from the root zone and transpiring via leaves into the air—can lower temperatures by ten degrees from surrounding areas—even when both areas are shaded. The trees contribute not only coolness, but also humidity. For example, the needles in an old coniferous forest can hold 264,000 gallons of water per acre—a shield of moisture important to other life-forms that must not dry out.

Trees also serve as air purifiers, absorbing pollutants through the porelike stomata in their leaves and breaking down troublesome chemicals into less harmful substances during photosynthesis. The U.S. Forest Service estimated that trees in Chicago annually remove 15 metric tons of carbon monoxide,

84 tons of sulfur dioxide, 191 tons of ozone, and 212 tons of particulates—all with only 11 percent of the city forested.

Tree-induced fog-drip, shade, and moisture are all important to the locales and the regions where trees grow, and even more important, forests are critical to the greater climate worldwide. Principally composed of the carbon they have taken from the atmosphere, trees store the element in solid form but release it again as gas when they decompose or burn. Tree loss through deforestation and fire accounts for 18 percent of global carbon dioxide emissions—the second-largest human-caused source, exceeded only by our burning of fossil fuels, which converts solid or liquid carbon to gaseous carbon dioxide. As this gas accumulates in the atmosphere, it traps heat with a "greenhouse effect" causing global warming. Atmospheric carbon dioxide has increased by more than 30 percent since the beginning of the industrial age. While existing carbon dioxide concentrations alone cause grave concern, scientists predict another 40 percent increase during the next sixty years. An eventual six-fold increase along with a rapid increase of other troublesome greenhouse gases—methane and nitrous oxide—is possible.

With the most prestigious panel of scientists assembled to deal with the topic, the United Nations Environment Programme has confirmed that global warming has begun and will accelerate. Scientists conservatively expect an average warming of 5.4 degrees Fahrenheit by the year 2055, a change that promises monumental disruptions to life.

For starters, the oceans will rise. In 2007 the Intergovernmental Panel on Climate Change predicted a sea level increase of ten to twenty-three inches this century owing only to the spatial expansion of water at higher temperatures. The added melting of ice caps could ultimately raise sea level as much as five feet, which would flood immense coastal areas including many cities. Warming will disable or transform agricultural and forest regions owing to heat and altered precipitation. The new climate will displace trees and other species from their home ranges faster than they can naturally migrate northward—ten times faster than any known rate of adjustment in the past. Forest fires will become more common and regeneration less complete. Warm-climate diseases, such as malaria, will increase, along with severe tropical storms, which are caused by super-warmed ocean water.

In the face of this global catastrophe, forests offer some hope. Half of the mass of trees is carbon, created through photosynthesis when the troublesome carbon dioxide in the atmosphere is absorbed; trees do precisely the opposite of what we inadvertently do when we burn fossil fuel and release carbon. One tree can absorb twenty-five to fifty pounds of carbon a year; an acre of forest can sequester ten tons. This cannot solve the problem of global warming, but by increasing tree cover—and letting trees get larger before they are cut—we can buffer the change while we begin to tackle the essential tasks of improving energy efficiency, switching to solar and wind power, and—most important—curbing population growth.

While living forests are crucial to reversing the trend in global warming, the same altered climate quietly kills the forests that we increasingly depend upon. Furthermore, as our need for carbon-sequestering forests increases, we continue to clear more and more land of trees. But before we look further at the perils that we and modern forests together face, let's consider the makeup of our varied regions of woodlands, and let's take time to really see both the trees and the forests that make America what it is.

Fire in ENGELMANN SPRUCE and LODGEPOLE PINE FOREST, Yellowstone National Park, Wyoming

Fires have been a part of forest ecosystems ever since forests began. Naturally caused by lightning, fires create clearings and burn dead vegetation and other fuel that accumulates on the ground. This recycles nutrients and stimulates many plants that are important to wildlife. Though this crown fire in 1988 burned to the top of several trees, most fires historically burned only close to the ground, leaving large trees intact. That pattern has been upset by the harvest of large trees, the overcrowded growth that results, and the attempts to suppress all fires, which ultimately result in hotter and larger fires.

***Overleaf:* WESTERN HEMLOCKS, GRAND FIRS, and TANOAKS in Humbug Mountain State Park, Oregon**

Conifers benefit from ample precipitation along the Pacific Northwest coast, where moisture, temperate climate, and low elevation together create the most productive tree-growing region on the continent.

CHAPTER FOUR

SYLVANIA

ENLIVENING THE GEOGRAPHY OF our country, trees fill every conceivable niche of suitable habitat, which includes most land with even a sprinkling of soil and a usual prerequisite of at least twenty inches of rain and fourteen frost-free weeks per year. The community of trees—whether shrubby mangroves in Florida or great conifers in the Northwest—determines not only the kinds of wildlife that will live underneath, but also why each region looks the way it does. Each forest type has its own style—its subtle hues of green, varying degrees of shade and openness, height of canopy, flashing warm colors in autumn, and individual abilities to cope with heat, cold, snow, storms, floods, drought, browsing animals, and insect pests. And in photographing trees throughout America, I found that each forest is its own art form.

The distinctions, however, are often blurred at the edges where one woodland type blends into another. Making sense of the mix, Robert G. Bailey of the U.S. Forest Service has mapped fifty-two ecoregions of the United States, showing where one type of vegetation ends and the next begins. With less detail, the popular field guide *Trees of North America* identifies ten major forest types, and I've adapted its taxonomy to select the seven portfolios of forest photos in this chapter. As I searched for the pictures, the regional character of each forest became evident. With camera in hand, I was constantly lured onward, anticipating the quintessential trees of each biome I explored.

I started in the Northern Forest, where New England, New York, and the northern Midwest showcase a mix of conifers and broadleaf trees. Near the Canadian border in Maine, a boreal forest of somber green is dominated by red, white, and black spruces, along with balsam firs. Just to the south lies a transitional belt of broadleaf trees called northern hardwoods, accompanied by the evergreen hemlocks and white pines. Paper birches stand out as if drawn with a white pencil on a dusky green backdrop. These are the woods of spectacular autumn color; beeches, maples, and birches brighten mountains, riverfronts, and lakeshores. Mostly wooded at the time of the Pilgrims, 80 percent of the Northeast was cleared for farmland, but today 80 percent is woodland again now that abandoned farmlands in this region once again support trees. They sprout

TANOAKS with REDWOODS, McWay Canyon, Julia Pfeiffer Burns State Park, California

RED OAK with WHITE OAKS, Maple Woods, near Kansas City, Missouri

up even in the middle of toppling stonewalls that once separated fields. To the west, the northern reaches of Michigan, Wisconsin, and Minnesota lie at the same latitudes as the Northeast. Though geographically Midwestern, they share a similar climate with the Northeast, and therefore the forests are similar as well.

The central hardwoods region, extending from New York to Georgia, is the largest woodland biome in the United States (but not in North America; the spruce-dominated boreal forest extending across Canada is larger). From the North Atlantic to the Great Plains, scores of deciduous tree species mingle together. Beeches and sugar maples mark the northern reaches and higher elevations. The Appalachian Mountains are covered with varied broadleaf woods like a woolly blanket shaken out and dropped gently over the aged hills. Oaks predominate on drier hillsides. Silver maples, birches, willows, and magnificent fat-trunk sycamores richly endow riversides.

The central hardwoods extend across the Midwest to the dry fringes of the Great Plains in an undulating front influenced for eons by rainfall, fire and, more recently, by clearing for farmland. Yet, in a few isolated preserves, the "Big Woods" of the original Midwest can still be found with groves of sugar maples, basswoods, oaks, and other hardwoods. The drier Ozark Mountains of Missouri and Arkansas feature oaks and hickories. Farther west, stately bur oaks and congregations of hackberries finger out into the prairie.

The mix of trees increases even more toward the south where the winters become milder; forty of the Central Hardwood species might share the high canopy of the Appalachians south of Virginia. Lacking the interruptions of continental glaciers in the past, this is among our oldest of forest types. In the Smoky Mountains, the "cove hardwood" community ranks as an exemplar of forest diversity with 130 tree species.

South of the central hardwoods, and extending along the coastal plain of the Atlantic and Gulf of Mexico, Southern Forests flourish on sandy hills and in spongy wetlands. Here striking baldcypresses tower with roots immersed in black swamp water. Draped in Spanish "moss" (*Tillandsia usneoides* is actually a flowering plant), live oaks preside over lowland sites near the coast, and pines cover the uplands. The southern end of Florida is subtropical; sable palms wave in the breeze above sandy beaches and wetlands.

Along with the central hardwoods, the Southern Forest ranks as the richest major woodland domain with 176–195 species of trees. However, through most of the region, grossly simplified industrial forests have replaced the natural ones. Loblolly pines once grew two hundred feet tall, but are now cultivated like corn in endless rows on commercial tree plantations and cut before they reach fifty feet. Logging has eliminated 98 percent of the tight-grained pine called longleaf, which has eighteen-inch needles. Once dressing ninety-two million acres from Virginia through Texas, this tree provided irreplaceable habitat for southern birds and wildlife.

Far to the west, an entirely different forest biome can be found in the Rocky Mountains. These reach high enough to accumulate deep snow, and therefore have their own distinctive evergreen forests. The species vary from valley to mountaintop; a hundred-foot rise in elevation causes the equivalent climatic change of zooming sixty miles north. Lodgepole pines sprout in the wake of fires, and quaking aspens brighten sunny slopes, especially in the southern Rockies. Higher up, Engelmann spruces dominate, followed by a belt of subalpine firs. At upper elevations, whitebark or limber pines brave winter storms. Near timberline—where the elevation or exposure is so severe that trees can't grow tall—gardens of miniature wind-sculpted trees are called krummholz.

Drylands occur both east and west of the Rockies. Grasslands of the Great Plains lie from the Midwest to the mountains, while desert and steppe country lies south and west of the Rockies. Together, these drylands account for most of the land in the West. Precipitation of less than twenty inches makes the growth of trees almost impossible. However, where mountains collect snow, scattered pinyon pines and junipers manage to take root. Some mountains reach high enough to capture deeper snow, which supports pockets of ponderosa pines and Douglas-firs on north-facing slopes. Timeless bristlecone pines find isolated habitat at high elevations. Throughout the Plains, and even in the deserts of the Southwest, cottonwoods and willows green the riverbanks if the flows have not been diverted for ranching, farming, or cities. Deep in the Southwest, saguaro cacti are emblematic of the Sonoran Desert, and across southeastern California, contorted arms of Joshua trees distinguish the Mojave Desert.

The Sierra Nevada of California is home to a stellar collection of great conifers—part of the greater biome of Pacific Coast Forest but considered separately in this chapter because the Sierra is a distinctive ecosystem with an amazingly photogenic repertoire of trees. Fantastic in their towering presence, humbling in their sunlit groves, the giant sequoias grow larger than any other trees in the world. Magnificent stands of ponderosa pines, Jeffrey pines, sugar pines, incense cedars, and red firs stand on the mid-and upper slopes of the great mountain range. Adjoining it, central and southern California have valley oaks five feet thick in elegant savannas.

The extraordinary arboreal province of the Northwest begins in northern California where the redwoods—the tallest trees in the world—master a thin belt just inland from the Pacific Ocean and extending northward to Oregon. Douglas-firs, grand firs, western hemlocks, and western redcedars reach their prime here in the world's greatest kingdom of conifers.

Forests in the northwestern Coast Ranges were never covered by glaciers, and with the resulting variety of trees—twenty-nine types of conifers alone—the Klamath and Siskiyou Mountains along the California-Oregon border are considered the western counterpart to the species-rich Great Smoky Mountains. Bigleaf and vine maples brighten rainy forests, and bay leaves scent the coastal woods with memorable pungency. Farther north, Washington's Olympic Peninsula ranks as a premier temperate rainforest; dripping mosses drape giant Sitka spruces, western hemlocks, and redcedars.

The Pacific Coast forest continues along the western slope of British Columbia and extends across southern Alaska to Kodiak Island, though owing to their remoteness, the Alaskan forests appear in this book as a separate portfolio. Like the coastal woods of Oregon and Washington, only colder, the northern rainforest arcs across a thousand miles of southern Alaska. Here, entire islands and valleys have been clearcut for log exports to Asia, but thanks to concerted efforts by conservationists, uncut forests also remain intact with acreage dwarfing that of forests found to the south.

In Alaska's north, a far-western extension of the boreal forest with black-and-white spruces is called the taiga. Eventually even miniature conifers, looking like bristly bottle brushes, give way to tundra where it is so cold with sap-freezing winters and armored with rock-hard permafrost that trees cannot take root or survive. Here in the Arctic, one stands face-to-face with the raw windy barrens of a land without trees.

Finally, rising as precious outposts in the Pacific, the Hawaiian Islands are soaked by rain-bearing trade winds and support tropical forests. With active volcanoes still spilling molten lava into the ocean, and with heavy runoff carving the land the way a sculptor might, these islands are still being formed, and as they take shape, entirely new forests are born.

The Northern Forest

PORCUPINE MOUNTAIN FOREST, **Michigan**

Sugar maples and yellow birches share the same ecological niche in Michigan's Porcupine Mountain Wilderness State Park—one of the largest tracts of eastern old-growth forest and an arboreal highlight of the upper Midwest.

MOUNT KEARSARGE, **New Hampshire**

Sugar and red maples turn orange and red across Appalachian foothills that stretch out toward the Atlantic Ocean. Taller white pines rise within this forest, and white spruce thicken lowlands in the background.

NORTH WOODS at Baxter State Park, Maine
Black spruces, white spruces, and balsam firs blanket hundreds of thousands of acres in northern Maine. Almost all of this region is owned by industrial timber companies, which cut the forest every thirty years. Baxter State Park is the largest area safeguarded from timber harvest. For wildlife to thrive, protected forest corridors are needed as linkages to other parklands of the region.

WOODLANDS at Acadia National Park, Maine
In this maritime coastal forest of the North, a trio of red oaks rises along with an eclectic mix of species including yellow-leaved beech trees and paper birches with white trunks.

WHITE PINES above the Lamoille River near Johnson, Vermont
Throughout New England and much of the Northeast, white pine forests were once prevalent with magnificent trees up to 240 feet tall. Virtually all were cut. New pines are maturing here on sunny slopes and flats that were farmed a century ago.

EASTERN HEMLOCKS, Ice Glen, Stockbridge, Massachusetts
Still gracing shady coves in the forests of New England, the eastern hemlock is dying out owing to an invasion of an exotic insect, the woolly adelgid, which advances from south-to-north and may kill most or all of these evergreens.

YELLOW BIRCH, Saco River, New Hampshire
Widespread throughout New England and the northern Appalachians, yellow birch trees have bark that curls in thin, tissuelike layers.

WINTER FOREST along the East Branch Pemigewasset River, White Mountain National Forest, New Hampshire
The bare trunks and limbs of paper birches and red maples stand out against the somber backdrop of red and white spruces, along with one tall white pine, identified by its drooping branches.

SUGAR MAPLE, northcentral Pennsylvania
With dazzling color, sugar maples are one of autumn's great visual feasts. These trees also act as "nutrient pumps" by pulling nutrients up from deep in the soil and depositing them on the surface of the ground as leaf litter, which benefits other plants and animals.

BEECH TREES along the West Branch Farmington River, Massachusetts
Beeches are a mainstay of northeastern forests, producing nuts favored by wildlife. These trees often appear with a dark green complement of eastern hemlocks, but both species are imperiled by blights caused by exotic pests.

SUGAR MAPLES and BEECH TREES along the West Branch Sacandaga River, New York
Spanning the Adirondack Mountains, the largest state park in America was protected through an amendment to the New York state constitution requiring that a large tract of forest be reserved as the source of water for cities and industries downstream. Here sugar maples have shed their autumn leaves and beeches have turned yellow and orange.

EASTERN WHITE PINES, Housatonic Meadows State Park, Connecticut
Once the dominant tree across New England, New York, and Pennsylvania, the white pine now grows in small groves but appears to be increasing in some areas. The soft needles and stately trunks make this tree a favorite of many people across its broad range.

BEECH TREE and the Pomperaug River, Connecticut
Though their natural range extends from Canada to Florida, beech trees have excelled in the north and on sandy, alluvial soils along rivers.

RED MAPLE, **Itasca State Park, Minnesota**
A bi-colored maple turns directly from summer green to fall crimson among speckled alder trees near the source of the Mississippi River. Red maples pioneer forests that have been cleared by fires, wetlands that have dried up, and tracts that have been cutover throughout the East. The red maple has one of the longest ranges of any tree, extending from Canada to the southern tip of Florida.

GOOSEBERRY FALLS STATE PARK, **Minnesota**
Northern white-cedars rise over a thicket of thimbleberries near the northwest coast of Lake Superior. Though rarely rising taller than sixty feet, white-cedars can live for several hundred years and provide important shelter for deer in winter. Moose, snowshoe hares, and cottontail rabbits eat the twigs and foliage while red squirrels and songbirds feast on the seeds of this evergreen.

FOREST and PRESQUE ISLE RIVER, **Michigan**
Northern white-cedars and eastern mountain maples overhang scoured-out potholes of the Presque Isle River near Lake Superior. One of the lesser-known maples, this one rarely achieves tree size and prefers rocky woods, ravines, and waterfronts. Its bark is gnawed by deer, moose, and beavers, and its buds are plucked by ruffed grouse.

AUTUMN in Porcupine Mountain Wilderness State Park, Michigan
Yellow birches, white ashes, and sugar maples glow with autumn color above multiple layers of eroded sandstone near Lake Superior.

SILVER MAPLES along the Mississippi River, Minnesota
In a broad range across the East and Midwest, silver maples keep streams and rivers cool by shading them from direct sunlight.

Overleaf: BRULE RIVER FOREST, northern Wisconsin
Light gray trunks of bigtooth aspens stand in contrast with the autumn color of red maples, yellow birches, and a young white spruce. All these trees colonize areas that have been burned.

Central Hardwoods and the Appalachians

AUTUMN LEAVES along the Pomperaug River, Connecticut
Leaves of the red oak, beech, sugar maple, tuliptree, and bigtooth aspen have fallen into a small wetland at the Bent of the River Nature Preserve near Southbury. The central hardwood forests extend from the southern Appalachians to sites such as this in southern New England.

CLOUD FOREST on Spruce Knob, West Virginia
Shrouded by a damp cloud in the humid atmosphere of the central Appalachians, birches, ashes, maples, oaks, hickories, and tuliptrees all mix together on the slopes of West Virginia's tallest mountain.

APPALACHIAN FOREST at Ohiopyle State Park, Pennsylvania
Four hues of autumn are seen here with red oaks in yellow and green, a chestnut oak in golden-brown, and a red maple in full fall color.

EASTERN WHITE PINES, Cook Forest State Park, Pennsylvania
Green algae color the trunk of a dead white pine and also a live one, while a small eastern hemlock and beech rise behind. Cook Forest was set aside as a state park after nearly all of Pennsylvania was logged.

YELLOW BIRCHES along Slippery Rock Creek, Pennsylvania
Common through much of the central and northern hardwoods belt, yellow birches do well along streams and on cool shaded slopes. Owing to the narrowness and resulting shade in this gorge, the forest is similar to what is found much farther north.

LATE-AUTUMN SNOWSTORM at the Youghiogheny River, Pennsylvania

In a wet October snowstorm, tuliptrees and beeches still hold onto their yellow leaves, and red maples are easily identified against a dark forest of hemlocks rising above the whitewater of the Youghiogheny River.

BLACK WALNUT in autumn, Pine Creek, Pennsylvania

Walnuts may be the most nutritious of all nuts in the forest. In autumn color, this young tree grows in front of a white ash and sycamores with mottled bark.

YOUNG CHESTNUT TREE, Mohonk Preserve, New York

Once dominant throughout eastern forests, growing to towering heights and producing enormous quantities of nutritious nuts for wildlife and people, chestnut trees were nearly exterminated in the early 1900s. But small shoots and saplings still grow from old, living root stocks. Though this photo was taken in New York, chestnuts once thrived throughout the central hardwoods region.

SYCAMORE **at Bernheim Forest, Kentucky**
Limbs reach out from a large sycamore, whose young, white bark will become mottled in green, brown, and gray as it flakes with age. Just south of Louisville, Bernheim Forest is an exquisite private preserve dedicated to education about forests and the environment.

HARDWOODS **along the Blue Ridge Parkway, Virginia**
A mixed group of oaks and other hardwoods has reached its peak color in October along the scenic drive that follows the crest of the Blue Ridge Mountains from Shenandoah National Park to the Great Smoky Mountains.

RED MAPLE, Santeetlah River valley, North Carolina
Fall colors are stunning throughout the Appalachians. Here a red maple is flanked by two smaller dogwoods with maroon leaves, tall tuliptrees, oaks, a white pine, and a sugar maple that has turned yellow.

CHOKE CHERRY at Humpback Rocks, Virginia
This small tree leafs-out early in the Appalachian spring. Behind it and still looking wintry, chestnut oaks are dampened by fog at the crest of the Blue Ridge Mountains.

Southern Appalachian forest of FRASER FIRS, Clingmans Dome, North Carolina

The stunning mix of southern Appalachian trees spreads out below the highest peak in the Great Smoky Mountains. The dead trees, however, are Fraser firs, which exist only on the high ridges of this park but are succumbing to an exotic insect and are hampered by air pollution from coal burning power plants in the Tennessee River basin.

TULIPTREES and blue sky, Joyce Kilmer Memorial Forest, North Carolina

Sometimes called yellow poplars, tuliptrees are fast-growing hardwoods and in many places are the tallest and largest trees in the eastern forest. While the rest of the region was heavily logged, this small backwoods enclave was passed over by neglect on the part of loggers. Later set aside for preservation, the grove was named in honor of the young man who wrote the poem "Trees" and was later killed in World War I.

AMERICAN BEECH, Sipsey Fork, Alabama

Though this tree remains healthy for now, beeches of the north are being decimated by an exotic insect from Europe that bores small holes in the bark, which are then infected by a fatal fungus. Blisters erupt on the trunks and worsen until they cover the tree and kill it. The pest is working its way through the Appalachians from north-to-south.

JOYCE KILMER MEMORIAL FOREST, North Carolina
A tangle of rhododendrons lies in front of a large tuliptree on the left, a mossy beech tree canted at an angle in the center, and a hemlock on the right, which is dying from the exotic woolly adelgid infestation.

TULIPTREES with a YELLOW BUCKEYE, Great Smoky Mountains, Tennessee

A yellow buckeye with fresh leaves stands in front of a tuliptree forest near the Little River. Also greening this April scene, a young yellow birch rises on the left and a sugar maple branches-out on the right.

APPALACHIAN FOREST south of the Great Smoky Mountains, North Carolina

A striped maple in yellow foliage is backed by the trunks of tuliptrees, with sugar maples and hemlocks in the background. Greenish twigs of the striped maple photosynthesize even in winter and are eagerly eaten by deer, rabbits, and other herbivores when food on the ground is covered with snow.

EASTERN SYCAMORE, Big Darby Creek, Ohio

A hearty sycamore grips onto a rocky streamside in winter. The most massive trees in the East, sycamores can reach six feet in diameter and often harbor hollowed-out cavities occupied by raccoons, swallows, wood ducks, or other wildlife.

BASSWOODS, SUGAR MAPLES, and RED OAKS, Hoosier National Forest, Indiana

Along the Little Blue River, this stand of hardwoods is recovering from past logging and may eventually become an old-growth forest once again.

RED and WHITE OAKS, Hemmer Woods, Indiana
At a small seventy-three-acre isolated grove, old oaks along with mockernut and shagbark hickories are surrounded by fields of corn and strip mines, but serve as a reminder of the once-great midwestern forest.

BLACK WALNUT trees, Gebhard Woods State Park, Illinois
Bearing the most nutritious nuts and some of the most valuable hardwood, black walnut trees loom large on this fertile site near the Illinois River. Sizeable nuts give the seeds of walnuts and hickories enough food stores to germinate in thick layers of leaves that typically cover the soil beneath the broadleaf canopy.

WHITE OAK at Wildcat Mountain State Park, Wisconsin
A white oak remains green long after neighboring sugar maples have turned yellow in southern Wisconsin. Because of high tannin content, the oak leaves will later fade to brown, and then they will adhere to the tree well into winter. Oaks yield bumper crops of acorns, which are a mainstay of deer, squirrels, and other wildlife. One oak can produce up to twenty-eight thousand acorns a year.

The South

WATER TUPELOS near Camden, South Carolina
Water tupelos abound in lowlands and can endure floodwaters for months at a time across wetlands of the South.

BLACK WILLOW, Altamaha River lowlands, Georgia
With dark, roughly textured bark, black willows are the largest among many willow species and can be found along riverfronts across much of the United States.

BALDCYPRESS TREES, **Congaree Swamp National Monument, South Carolina**

The baldcypress is the signature tree of southeastern swamps, but owing to logging and to drainage of wetlands, large trees are now rare. The Congaree Swamp National Monument offers one of the finest examples of coastal plain old-growth in the South.

CHICKASAWHATCHEE **Wildlife Management Area, Georgia**
Water tupelo leaves cover the water at this central Georgia swamp. Tupelos and baldcypresses stand in the water while poison ivy vines climb the trees in search of more sunlight.

Overleaf: LIVE OAKS **and** SAW PALMETTOS, **Cumberland Island, Georgia**
In a showcase of tropical-style vegetation, palmettos fill the understory at Cumberland Island while live oaks spread their canopies across sandy hummocks within a quarter-mile of the Atlantic shore. Living for several centuries, these are the broadest crowned of all oaks.

SAW PALMETTOS and SWEETGUM, Alexander Springs, Florida

Sunlight catches the star-shaped leaves of a young sweetgum along with trunks of sable palms (far right) and redbays in a break of saw palmettos. A part of Ocala National Forest, this tropical-style woodland borders a spring of crystal clear water with ten-foot alligators, slender gar, and a host of waterfowl.

SABLE PALMS and LIVE OAK, Myakka River State Park, Florida
Just above the grassy sweep of riverfront wetlands, sable palms and an old live oak bathe in the warm evening light of southwestern Florida.

LONGLEAF PINE GROVE, **Highlands Hammock State Park, Florida**
Once covering much of the South, longleaf pines grew with diameters of three-and-a-half feet. A choice lumber of the South, their fine grain was prized for many uses. Only token tracts of the native longleaf forests remain, but state and federal agencies as well as conservancies and some private landowners are trying to restore this keystone species.

BALSAM TORCHWOOD **in southcentral Florida**
This small and inconspicuous tree of southern swamplands is shaded among ferns and other epiphytes clinging to its trunk in Highlands Hammock State Park. In southern Florida, hammocks are elevated limestone domes where forests of up to seventy species are able to reach maturity because they are protected from frequent fires by surrounding wetlands. Dense cover also safeguards the forest from occasional frosts that kill isolated trees.

EASTERN GRAY SQUIRREL in an ATLANTIC WHITE-CEDAR TREE, northern Florida

Seven species of American squirrels live in trees, and they all depend upon forests for every aspect of their lives. Eastern gray squirrels of the South often have a reddish cast, like this one near the Suwannee River.

LONGLEAF PINES, Talladaga National Forest, Alabama

Longleaf pines are critical to wildlife including the now-rare red-cockaded woodpecker, which constructs its cavity-nests in the trunks of the trees once they get large enough. This longleaf forest in the hill country of east-central Alabama is being managed for recovery by the Forest Service. Autumn colors of flowering dogwoods and red maples fill the background.

BALDCYPRESS and WATER TUPELO, **Manatee Springs, Florida**
Baldcypresses form buttresses, which may help stabilize the trees in chronically flooded sites along rivers, lakes, wetlands, and springs. Coastal baldcypress forests provide an effective buffer that protects inland landscapes and cities against tropical winds and storm surges, but the great trees are still being clearcut for chipping as garden mulch.

SABLE PALMS, **Myakka River State Park, Florida**
While many of the palms seen in Florida are introduced from elsewhere, the sable palms are native throughout the state. Among the oldest flowering plants in the fossil record, palms lack annual growth rings; except for an outer shell, the trunk is all living tissue.

Rocky Mountains

ENGELMANN SPRUCES, **Rabbit Ears Pass, Colorado**
Deep in the snows of February, and ready for the next approaching storm, these Engelmann spruces grow on mountain slopes while rolling wet meadows stretch out below them. Seedlings are able to survive in the dark shade of their parents, and so the spruces become climax stands—regenerating more of their kind over and over again without competition from other trees.

ENGELMANN SPRUCES and NARROWLEAF COTTONWOODS, Moose, Wyoming
The sun rises behind a riverfront forest along the Snake River. Riparian habitat is the most important for wildlife but comprises only about 5 percent of the American landscape.

ASPEN GROVE, South Fork of the White River, Colorado
Aspens are a staple in the diet of many wildlife species. Beavers and porcupines eat the bark. Buds and catkins are important winter food for grouse. Twigs, leaves, and bark are relished by rabbits and deer. The fresh teeth marks of elk are often seen on the trunks of trees after a long winter.

NARROWLEAF COTTONWOODS, Gros Ventre River, Wyoming
A keystone tree of the Rocky Mountains, cottonwoods depend on the natural flows of rivers. Upstream from the village of Kelly, a forest of varied-age trees reflects the occurrence of cyclical floods that are essential to germination. Vigorous cottonwood groves are an indication of healthy riparian systems.

LODGEPOLE PINES along the upper Salmon River, Idaho
On the warm, south-facing side of the river, heat, dryness, and occasional fires prevent most trees from replacing the ubiquitous sagebrush, but these lodgepole pines tap groundwater along the river and enjoy protection from fire in a cool and moist microclimate at the water's edge.

LODGEPOLE PINE snags, Beartooth Mountains, Montana
Burned just the year before, this forest readily grew a crop of red fireweed, a suite of native grasses and wildflowers that sprouted in the wake of the flames, and tiny pine seedlings that germinated soon after lodgepole cones popped open in the fire's heat. A new forest will rapidly replace the old, and in the meantime, nutritious, fire-dependent plants are a boon to local wildlife.

ENGELMANN SPRUCES and the Gallatin River, Montana
While ice crystallizes across the Gallatin River, a forest of Engelmann spruces darkens the shorelines and mountain slopes.

ASPENS in light snowfall, Blacktail Butte, Wyoming
Deciduous trees that need a new crop of leaves each year are at a marked disadvantage here where the winter might last seven months. Nonetheless thriving in the snow zone, aspens have chlorophyll in their bark, which enables them to photosynthesize before the leaves unfurl. This scene in Grand Teton National Park was photographed with a long exposure during a snowstorm that made the sky appear foggy.

Snowstorm in a LODGEPOLE PINE FOREST, Medicine Bow Mountains, northern Colorado
Well-adapted to their climate, these lodgepole pines have the ability to bend under heavy snowloads and survive even after being flattened or forced into contorted shapes throughout the winter. The lodgepole pine is the third-most plentiful tree in the West, following the Douglas-fir and ponderosa pine.

Drylands and Deserts

PETRIFIED WOOD, Theodore Roosevelt National Park, North Dakota

A rocky reminder of the distant past, this stump of petrified wood near the Little Missouri River indicates that large trees once grew on today's prairies.

Rainbow and NETLEAF HACKBERRY TREES, Green Memorial Wildlife Area, Kansas

West of the Mississippi, the Great Plains begin where rainfall decreases to less than twenty inches per year, which is generally the minimum needed for a forest. Summer thunderstorms, like the one that preceded this early morning rainbow, provide welcome moisture at the edge of the prairie. Throughout the drylands west of here, opportunistic trees appear mainly along streams or where snowfall accumulates on mountains.

SINGLELEAF PINYON **at Fisher Towers, Utah**

Adapted to heat and aridity, pinyon pines manage to flourish in some parts of the desert where no other trees except junipers can. Pinyons produce the finest nuts of all the pines and have long been a staple in the diets of southwestern Indians. Often associated with these pines, a Utah juniper grows to the left.

FREMONT COTTONWOOD **along the Green River, Utah**

In the arid West, several species of cottonwoods guard the shorelines of rivers and streams where the trees are able to sink their roots down to precious groundwater.

GAMBEL OAK near Moab, Utah
These tenacious small oaks—common in the drylands and Rocky Mountain foothills—find the water they need by tapping deep underground supplies in the red-rock canyons of the Colorado River.

SINGLELEAF PINYON in the East Humboldt Range, Nevada
With a bleached skeleton stripped bare by wind and weather, this pinyon may have been dead for hundreds of years on its high-elevation perch southwest of Wells.

PONDEROSA PINES, **Ochoco Mountains, central Oregon**
Rising from a dry volcanic steppe that lies in the rain shadow of the Cascade Range, the Ochoco Mountains reach high enough to rake significant snowfall from passing storms and to support ponderosa pines. These trees have the greatest range of any pine in the West, in part owing to root systems that can reach down as much as thirty-six feet and out for a hundred feet around the trunk. The needles are thick, enabling them to resist the desiccating effects of drought.

BRISTLECONE PINE, **White Mountains, California**
On high mountains where insect pests, fire, and flooding pose few threats, gnarled, wind-blasted bristlecone pines grow slowly. They are the oldest trees on earth.

SAGUARO CACTI, Organ Pipe Cactus National Monument, Arizona
Sun-drenched saguaro cacti prevail in the desert climate by storing great quantities of water and minimizing evaporative losses. Many of these charismatic cacti are dying from unknown causes. Also sharing this parched plain are deciduous blue palo verde trees and organpipe cacti with multiple stems.

SINGLELEAF PINYONS, Westgard Pass, California
Pinyon pines dot the flanks of the White Mountains where they receive light precipitation downwind from the Sierra Nevada.

JOSHUA TREES, **Joshua Tree National Park, California**
Firey sunsets illumine the desert of southern California where Joshua trees—bristly tall members of the yucca family—raise contorted arms to the sky.

CALIFORNIA FAN PALMS, **Anza-Borrego Desert State Park, California**
Revealing the presence of springs in an austere desert, California fan palms, also called Washingtonia, create an oasis that's essential to local wildlife. Native bunchgrasses—grazed to oblivion throughout much of their range—cluster in the foreground here at America's second-largest state park.

Sierra Nevada and Southern California

VALLEY OAK, **Kings River, California**
From foothills to high peaks, the Sierra Nevada is a mountain range of strikingly beautiful forests. Bright with the surge of life in springtime, these valley oaks reign over a steep-sloped savanna through the lower canyons of the Kings River.

SIERRA JUNIPER, **northern Sierra Nevada, California**
Living as long as three thousand years, junipers at high elevations in the Sierra can reach six feet in diameter though they may be shorter than twenty feet. With twisted trunks and branches, the persistent trees wrap their roots around rocks and anchor themselves in some of the harshest windswept and storm-ridden locations.

PONDEROSA PINES, San Joaquin River basin, California
Ponderosa pines grow here in a mature grove at the rim of the San Joaquin River canyon near Balloon Dome. Smaller incense cedars with vertically striated bark grow among the pines. This type of clear understory beneath huge trees once typified much of the western coniferous forest before the big trees were cut and frequent natural ground fires were suppressed.

WATER BIRCH along North Fork Big Pine Creek
Heavy snows from previous years have nearly flattened some of these flexible and now-prostrate water birch in a forested canyon at the eastern slope of the Sierra Nevada.

GIANT SEQUOIA with SUGAR PINES and WESTERN HEMLOCKS, Calaveras Big Trees State Park, California
Sequoias reach diameters exceeding thirty feet. Their bark is fire and insect resistant, and their vascular structure is such that lightning simply knocks the top off and does not travel down the trunk of the tree.

GIANT SEQUOIAS and PACIFIC DOGWOOD, **Calaveras Big Trees State Park, California**
Giant sequoias of the Sierra Nevada are the largest trees in the world. This Calaveras grove is safeguarded in a state park. Some of the finest big-tree groves are in Giant Sequoia National Monument, set aside for protection in the southern Sierra by President Bill Clinton in 2000. Those forests are threatened once again by Forest Service logging plans; large conifers around the sequoias would be cut, possibly exposing the big trees to wind damage.

WHITEBARK PINES, **Kennedy Creek basin, central Sierra Nevada, California**
Specializing in upper elevations where high winds and heavy snows are common, whitebark pines have branches that are so pliable they can be tied into knots when young. Owing to a warming climate, mountain pine beetles have reached epidemic levels and threaten many whitebark groves across the West.

LODGEPOLE PINES **and moonrise, Sonora Pass, California**

One of the more protean trees, lodgepoles grow as elegant conifers with finely textured bark in the Sierra Nevada but also in dense, matchstick-straight masses on fire-burned slopes in the Rockies and as wind-sculpted "shore pines" on the Pacific coast. Lodgepoles of many ages as well as whitebark pines share a common snowbank here at ten thousand feet in the Sierra.

RED FIRS, WHITEBARK PINES **and** MOUNTAIN HEMLOCKS **on Basin Peak, north of Donner Pass, California**

Several evergreens excel at high Sierra elevations where twelve feet of compacted snow lies on the ground by the end of winter. Though these trees are small, and will remain stunted at their exposed site, red firs in sheltered locations reach diameters of eight feet.

VALLEY OAK and sunrise south of Junipero Serra Peak, California
Among nineteen oak species in California, valley oaks are the largest, reaching five feet in diameter. One of the finest savannas of these giant hardwoods lies in a remote valley of the Santa Lucia Range west of King City. One hundred bird and sixty mammal species use oak trees of one kind or another in California.

LODGEPOLE PINES at Big Pine Creek, California
While morning shadows are cast by eastward spires of the Sierra, lodgepole pines grip onto the domes and granitic soils of these mountains.

VALLEY OAKS in the Sierra Nevada foothills, California
Valley oaks highlight a grassland savanna throughout the western Sierra foothills where granite bedrock juts out of the ground and lupine flowers bloom in the early spring.

SIERRA JUNIPER in winter, California
Even in the Sierra Nevada—a relatively well-protected landscape—75 percent of the original forest has been cut. This aged western juniper has escaped logging and—along with lodgepole pines—takes advantage of snowmelt along the North Fork Stanislaus.

The Northwest

JEDEDIAH SMITH REDWOODS State Park, California
Many of the largest redwoods, such as these at Stout Grove, rise from valley bottoms where river-deposited silt makes productive soil. Adapted to flooding, the trees will send out a new layer of roots when the old ones become covered by mud. The bark and wood are resistant to rot in the wet coastal climate. Fire and lightning are rare in the moist groves, and surrounding trees and rugged topography protect the redwoods from wind. Logging is the chief hazard; 95 percent of the ancient trees have been cut.

REDWOODS along the Damnation Creek Trail, northern California
Living in cool, foggy pockets of habitat from the central California coast to southern Oregon, redwoods are the tallest trees on earth. Many here in Del Norte Coast Redwoods State Park reach heights of three hundred feet or more.

BIGLEAF MAPLES and REDWOODS, Humboldt Redwoods State Park, California
With their creamy green flowers in springtime, bigleaf maples bloom at the sunlit edge of a redwood forest along Bull Creek—one of the finest big-tree groves.

GRAND FIR, **Port Orford Heads State Park, Oregon**
An aged grand fir along with Douglas-firs show some of the classic characteristics of an old-growth forest: large trees, broken limbs, standing dead snags with cavities for birds and small mammals, and veteran trees mixed with younger ones.

ROOSEVELT ELK, **Prairie Creek Redwoods State Park, California**
Largest of several subspecies of elk, the Roosevelt elk is a native of the Coast Range of California and Oregon. It lives in forests and meadowlands, and eats twigs and bark of trees as well as grass and herbs. Elk were once the most widespread hoofed animal in America, but owing to logging of forests, farming and grazing of prairies, and land development, they have been restricted to a small portion of their original range.

REDWOODS and PACIFIC RHODODENDRON, **northern California**
With an understory of blossoming Pacific rhododendron, big trees tower skyward in Del Norte Coast Redwoods State Park. Several state parks and the Redwood National Park protect many of the finest remaining groves of the giant trees.

BREWER SPRUCE, Siskiyou Mountains, California
The rare Brewer spruce, with weeping foliage, is found only in isolated pockets among the mountains of northern California and southern Oregon. Having thin bark, it is susceptible to fire damage but survives on rocky ridges and northern faces that seldom burn. Douglas-firs appear with the rare conifer here on Sanger Peak.

SISKIYOU MOUNTAINS, northern California and southern Oregon
Once connected geologically to the Sierra Nevada, and now bridging the Cascade and Coast ranges, the Siskiyou Mountains host plantlife from all three mountain masses. This region of temperate climate and topographic extremes was never glaciated, and so its forests continued to evolve without interruption by the continental ice sheets. Supporting twenty-nine species of conifers, the botanically rich ecosystem is seen here where the Smith River basin drops down to the ocean near Crescent City, California.

OREGON WHITE OAKS east of Ashland, Oregon
Oak woodlands are among the most important habitats for birds and wildlife, yet they are also the most endangered owing to land development in the lower elevations of the Cascades and other Pacific Coast mountain ranges.

VINE MAPLE along the Rogue River, Oregon
Named for its habit of sometimes pushing stems out across the ground before rising up to catch the light, the vine maple is often unnoticed among giant conifers and statuesque bigleaf maples, but in the autumn it's the brightest tree in the northwestern forest.

SITKA SPRUCES, Cape Lookout, Oregon
Crowning the coastal forest, Sitka spruces range from the Eel River in northern California to the outermost woodlands on Kodiak Island, Alaska. They do their best, however, along the coasts of Oregon and Washington.

PACIFIC MADRONE above the Rogue River, Oregon
Glossy with rainfall, a Pacific madrone extends its smooth-bark limbs in front of a canyon live oak. Both overlook the Rogue River, which is brown with the flood-flows of winter. Thriving near the Pacific coast, madrones can tolerate a wide range of 15 to 150 inches of rainfall a year.

SITKA SPRUCES at **Boardman State Park, Oregon**

Sitka spruces not only tolerate the high winds of the Pacific shoreline, but need salt spray from the ocean, which contains magnesium. These impressive, full-bodied conifers are found almost at the high-tide line and generally appear inland for only a few hundred yards. A hearty little shore pine also catches the sunlight here.

CONIFERS at **Lake of the Woods, Oregon**

Sunset's last glow warms a Douglas-fir, on the right, along with a grand fir, western white pine, and western hemlocks at the edge of a Cascade Mountain lake.

DOUGLAS-FIRS at **Opal Creek, Oregon**

Morning sun angles in on Douglas-firs with a western redcedar squeezing between them and Pacific rhododendrons in the foreground. After a protracted battle through the 1990s to halt logging in the Opal Creek watershed, this outstanding old-growth forest was protected.

WHITE ALDERS, **Nisqually River floodplain, Washington**

Alder trees spring up in great throngs when land is exposed to sun after fires or logging, and they specialize on floodplains. Filling an important function in the forest, the alders add nitrogen to the soil by hosting microbes in their rootmasses. These convert atmospheric nitrogen, which is plentiful, into soil-based nitrogen, which is in short supply but essential to plantlife.

DOUGLAS-FIRS **in the snow, Mt. Hood, Oregon**

Towering high, Douglas-firs can reach three hundred feet and live for eight hundred years. They do well in wet-to-moderately dry soils of the Pacific Coast ranges, the high mountains of the interior West, and the Rockies. This species is the mainstay of the northwestern timber industry.

VINE MAPLE at the Ohanapecosh River, Washington
Never getting much taller than forty feet, and often shrublike, vine maples add color to the forest. The buds, flowers, and leaves are used by many birds and mammals including squirrels, which store the seeds for winter food.

CONIFER FOREST and Mount Olympus, Washington
Western and mountain hemlocks, western white pines, whitebark pines, Douglas-firs, and Pacific silver firs cover the higher mountains of Olympic National Park. At lower elevations, this park has some of the most magnificent ancient forests on the West Coast.

WESTERN HEMLOCKS and GRAND FIRS at the Wind River, Washington

This mature grove at the Thornton T. Munger Research Natural Area is one of few uncut forests remaining in the Cascade Mountains of southern Washington.

SUBALPINE FIRS, **Mount Rainier, Washington**

With the widest distribution of any timberline tree in North America, subalpine firs taper in narrow, pointed shapes that efficiently shed snow and allow the trees to endure extreme conditions. A few mountain hemlocks also appear here with the firs.

Alaska and Hawaii

BALSAM POPLAR and BROWN BEARS, Katmai National Park, Alaska
Balsam poplars extend farther north than any other trees on the continent, even germinating on floodplains of rivers that flow toward the Arctic Ocean. Brown bears like to scratch the bark of these trees, as this sow is doing while guarding her cubs. A shrubby Sitka alder stands behind the broken poplar snag.

BLACK and WHITE SPRUCES, Mentasta Mountains, Alaska
For hundreds of miles across interior Alaska, black-and-white spruces form taiga—North America's boreal forest of small conifers. Permafrost prevents trees from getting large or from germinating where meltwater sits on top of ice that lies just a few feet underground. As global warming thaws the permafrost, trees become unstable, tilt, and fall over.

SITKA SPRUCES and BLACK HUCKLEBERRIES, **Admiralty Island, Alaska**
Sitka spruces tower up in extensive forests along the southeast coast of Alaska, while massive Alaska-cedars, western hemlocks, and mountain hemlocks thrive in the rainy belt of mountains just inland. Large parts of these forests have been cut owing to lucrative federal subsidies when logs from the Tongass National Forest are harvested and shipped to Asia. Admiralty Island is one of the important reserves that was protected as a national monument by President Jimmy Carter.

SITKA SPRUCES, **Kodiak Island, Alaska**

The range of the Sitka spruce reaches farther west than any other tree on mainland America. This forest is slowly colonizing land that was once covered by glaciers and now supports grasses, forbs, and berry bushes.

COCONUT PALMS with an understory of NAUPAKA,
Alahaka Bay, Hawaii
A tropical breeze bends the long trunks of coconut palms, which are adapted to hurricane-force winds. Wave-eroded coral has washed up as white cobbles on the black lava bedrock; this island is still being formed by eruptions of molten rock.

O HI A LEHUA TREE, **Kalopa State Park, Hawaii**
At one of few protected forests on the island of Hawaii, native trees are recovering in stands reminiscent of the impressive forests that predated Europeans' arrival. The o hi a lehua is one of the largest native trees, seen here with an `ie`ie vine clinging to its bark. Tree ferns, called hapu`u, stand to the left and right of the large tree.

KOA FOREST, **Mauna Loa Road, Hawaii**
Native koa appear at middle elevations on the island of Hawaii in splendid pocket groves. At lower elevations, nearly all native trees have been displaced by exotic tropical species introduced by settlers during the past two hundred years. With the loss of Hawaii's native plantlife, indigenous wildlife species have gone extinct as well.

COCONUT PALM and KIAWE TREE, **Spencer Beach Park, island of Hawaii**
Coconut palms were introduced to Hawaii by some of the earliest Polynesian settlers and have naturalized on many of the islands' beaches. The locust-like kiawe trees originated from one seed planted in 1828 and now cover whole savannas running for miles.

TREE FERN, or HAPU`U, **Hawaii Volcanoes National Park**
Along the Thurston Lava Tubes Trail, tree ferns reach high and their giant fiddleheads of new leaves begin to unravel in the springtime.

KOA FOREST, **Mauna Loa Road, Hawaii Volcanoes National Park**
One of few Hawaiian native trees that's still plentiful, koa populate dense groves where they've been protected from logging.

CHAPTER FIVE

REMNANTS AND REGROWTH

Seeking the finest arboreal visions I could imagine, and being open to surprises all along the path as I took pictures for this book, I immersed myself in forests in ways that felt comforting yet vital, satisfying yet stimulating. I explored new places, saw new sights, and learned new truths about the land and its life. I had looked forward to all of this, and the rewards were great. But I never expected that I'd be saying good-bye to so much that I had known and cared about ever since I was a child.

The eastern hemlock was always a favorite tree of mine. Slightly asymmetrical, it grew on cool, shaded slopes and along streams in the wild woods where I grew up. When I made fires for cooking at campsites, I sought out fallen hemlock limbs because pencil-size branches split when they broke, exposing dry, flammable wood inside even when it was raining. The limber-branched evergreen with its lacy texture of needles had always brightened the gray of winter and then complemented the lightness of summer woodlands with an enriching darkness. Charismatic, dependable, and beautiful, these conifers were like old friends of mine.

With great joy, I roamed beneath towering hemlocks on my very first trip to an ancient, uncut woods: Pennsylvania's Cook Forest State Park. Decades later, when I sought out the world's largest eastern hemlock in the Great Smoky Mountains, I was deeply grateful for the chance to stand next to the aged tree, and to simply touch it. Though it was getting dark, I did not want to leave its side, somehow feeling that I would never be able to return.

The hemlocks are now dying. Severe infestations of woolly adelgid—a minute insect introduced to this country from Asia—plague these trees throughout the central and southern Appalachians. Leaving fuzzy white tufts on the undersides of branches, the pest can kill its host within a few years. The enchanting groves in Whiteoak Canyon of Shenandoah National Park—a place where I'd found refuge on weekend escapes from college in Washington, D.C.—are now reduced to rotting gray snags. The great forest of Ramsey's Draft in Virginia is standing dead. The hemlocks of the Joyce Kilmer Grove in North Carolina are dying, their needle-bare twigs and branches turning the magnificent stands there into a ghost forest. The adelgid will likely spread to the champion tree I saw in the Smokies. After all the centuries it's been through, that great tree is unlikely to die a natural death, owing to ignorance, to carelessness, and an unacknowledged biological tragedy of globalism. It appears that few, if any of the hemlocks are resistant to the blight. And some creatures are far more affected than I. A few species of warblers nest only in these evergreens, and one survey found that 96 percent of the beautifully singing wood thrushes nested in them. When I photograph the remaining hemlocks, my feelings of appreciative joy are overcome with utter despair.

Blights have already killed off the American chestnut—the keystone tree of the East until a fungus from China eliminated virtually all the native trees by the 1920s. Chestnuts had been the forest's very finest food for wildlife and people, and accounted for one in three trees through much of the Appalachians. Then, in mid-century, we lost 95 percent of the American elms with their umbrella-like elegance, unmatched for street-tree beauty until the Dutch elm disease took its grim toll. (There is some hope: disease-resistant elms have been found among the survivors.) American beeches—another mainstay of the eastern forests—are now dying from an exotic fungus, *Nectria coccina*, that advances from north-to-south. Ash trees are severely infected by the emerald ash borer, sugar maples are dying in unusual numbers because of an exotic insect called pear thrips, and the list goes on.

Just as my grandfather, living literally at the base of Chestnut Ridge in the Appalachian Mountains of southwestern Pennsylvania, would not have imagined a forest without chestnuts, and just as my father would not have imagined a landscape without elms, I have a difficult time imagining a world without hemlocks and beeches. But anyone who looks can't help but see that these keystone species are dying en masse. With each loss, the forest becomes more biologically simplified, more impoverished. It supports less wildlife and becomes more susceptible to invasive plants. And without these great trees, the forest that we will see—even next year—will be less beautiful than the one we see today.

These current crises in the woods reflect only the latest in a long history that spans several hundred years of logging, soil depletion, air pollution, unnatural fire suppression, and urban development. Now, exotic pests are abetted by weaknesses imposed by all the other accumulated changes. For example, soil damaged by careless logging makes a tree less able to gain the

DYING HEMLOCKS, Joyce Kilmer Memorial Forest, North Carolina
Much of the whitish cast to this "ghost" forest owes to the dead and dying branches, twigs, and foliage of eastern hemlocks that are infected with the exotic woolly adelgid. The insect will kill most or all of the hemlocks in the East.

nourishment it needs to fight off invisible attacking forces, such as fungal diseases from other parts of the world.

To understand the complexity of forces affecting modern forests in America, the challenges to their future, and their ultimate fate, it's first important to know that nearly all the original trees were cut down.

The clearing of farmland and logging of areas that never grew back has reduced the forested expanse of the United States by about a third since European settlement began. The reduction lies principally in the East and Midwest where 280 million acres are now cultivated for crops. Forests have also been replaced by the sprawl of cities; in temperate America, these were all once dense woodlands. The acreage covered by trees reached its nadir in 1920, and then began to increase as eastern farmlands were retired, but losses are now mounting once again owing to suburbanization fed by rapid population growth. Furthermore, the one-third-reduction figure covers only the forest that was cut and never allowed to recover. Nearly all the rest was cut as well.

All across America, logging has occurred almost everywhere trees can live—certainly on the 15 percent of forest land that's owned by the timber industry, and also on the 28 percent that's in public ownership, and the remaining 57 percent held by individuals. Even in the Sierra Nevada—a relatively safeguarded mountain range with some big national parks—75 percent of the original forest was logged.

Nationwide, and especially in the West, much of the residual uncut forest can be found in the national parks and national forests. The parks are well protected but account for only about 3 percent of the American landscape. Covering 8 percent of America, the national forests were established for woodland and watershed protection and management, but only one in ten of those 191 million federal acres have escaped the saw—mostly at high elevations representing the least productive and least diverse forest types. Nationwide, less than 5 percent of our total original old-growth remains, and only half of that is safeguarded by wilderness or park designations, according to *Defining Sustainable Forestry*. We're down to mere remnants, and unfortunately, what's left is severely handicapped by fragmentation—reduction to small parcels that aren't large enough to sustain the full mix of native wildlife. Furthermore, lacking neighboring trees, these isolated acres are subject to wind damage and are easily infiltrated by exotic plants and diseases.

Outside the protected reserves, timber companies have harvested many forests a second, third, and fourth time. Logging can be done well—and is by some people—but too often it causes soil loss, watershed damage, herbicide pollution, decreased species diversity, and oversimplified monocultures of cash-crop trees called "plantations."

Old-growth forests take a lot of time to develop—175 years, for example, to establish a large Douglas-fir on the West Coast, followed by many more decades for plants and animals to weave together their intricate ecological relations. In drier climates, forests need even longer. But many low-elevation tracts in the West are now harvested every sixty years. Appalachian forests tend to be cut every forty to one hundred years, and pulpwood-mowing machines crunch through whole geographies in the North Woods and South on a thirty-year cycle or less. The timber may bring a good-enough price to continue this process for awhile, but the circle of life that the old forest had served is gone. No one knows how many years such frequent cutting can continue without the forest failing to effectively recover, though the time is almost certainly limited. Chronic losses are already evident: red fir forests fail to regenerate on the mowed and over-heated slopes of the Sierra Nevada; stunted oaks struggle in depleted soils of the repeatedly cut Appalachians.

Excessive or careless logging not only eliminates the old trees but destroys the very life systems that are essential for new generations. As early as 1864 George Perkins Marsh, in *Man and Nature*, warned about what happened when earlier civilizations in the Mediterranean and Middle East had denuded their forests. The soil's fertility was depleted, or the soil washed completely away. The famed Cedars of Lebanon never grew back. Warnings of ecosystem collapse have multiplied as we've learned more about forest ecology. Now we know that soil is lost in both subtle ways and in wholesale slabs; at the Siuslaw National Forest in Oregon, all but 27 of 245 landslides following a heavy storm were traced to logging and logging roads. Without soil, there can be no forest.

Entire species have become endangered because of comprehensive cutting. The ivory-billed woodpecker, which virtually disappeared with the loss of the last big oak and tupelo

CLEARCUT near the Umpqua River, Oregon
This Douglas-fir forest is being clearcut without regard to steep slopes, watercourses, soil erosion, or wildlife habitat. All but 5 percent of the Oregon Coast Range and all but 10 percent of the old-growth in the West has been cut, and now much of the land is being cut again. Poor state laws regarding timber harvest fail to adequately protect rivers, watersheds, and a wide array of native plants and wildlife.

forests in the 1940s, had depended on southern old-growth where it lived on insects routed from aged trees. The long-lost bird was reportedly sighted again in 2005 and—if alive—is dependent on the protection and expansion of mature forests in southern wetlands. Suffering a similar fate, the red-cockaded woodpecker barely survives in rare longleaf pine stands of the South. Other species requiring old-growth include sleek fur bearers called the fisher and the marten, the northern goshawk, the spotted owl, and the northern red-legged frog. The loss of old forests means a loss of these creatures and others in patterns that reverberate the whole way through the food chain.

While clearcuts can be ugly, and expose soils to erosion, new trees in the years that follow often appear healthy and may, in fact, be growing fast. But the middle-aged forests, ten-to-one hundred years old, can be the least valuable for wildlife and species diversity. These forests lack a mixed understory, sun-lit openings that result from individual old trees toppling over, large fallen logs, and standing snags that house whole families of creatures. Yet this kind of monoculture is precisely what many production-oriented foresters want. To make way for their commercial crop, they routinely poison hardwoods such as hickory, pawpaw, and persimmon in the South—all critical foods for wildlife. In these market-driven tracts, the trees all look about the same, and because they *are* about the same, the trees in plantations succumb to disease far more frequently than do forests with a mix of species. This means that even more

FRASER FIRS, **Great Smoky Mountains National Park, North Carolina and Tennessee**

Weakened by severe air pollution from coal-burning power plants in the Tennessee Valley, Fraser firs are now being killed by the exotic balsam woolly adelgid. As survivors of the last ice age, these trees appear only in a small pocket of high-elevation terrain in the southern Appalachians but are likely to go extinct in the wild.

pesticides are needed in an escalating chemical battle—one where birds and fish are inevitably the big losers.

Controversies about the overcutting of forests have raged in many parts of the country, hitting an especially high pitch in the West and the Northeast.

Conflicts over logging on national forests throughout the West have brewed for decades. Confronted with a storm of protest about clearcutting on federal land, Congress passed the National Forest Management Act in 1976. This barred cutting in national forests where irreversible damage would result, required protection of species diversity, and called for management plans. But with a change of politics—from President Carter to President Reagan—reform hit the wall. Heavily influenced by the timber industry, the new plans called for far more cutting than ever.

The General Accounting Office struck a sensitive fiscal nerve by showing that timber sales on national forest land didn't make money for the government. Instead, they cost the Forest Service and taxpayers half a billion dollars per year. In the Southwest alone, the subsidized program taxed Americans twenty-four thousand dollars a year for each timber-industry job—public dollars spent helping corporations to liquidate ancient forests that belong to all Americans.

Even where the Forest Service indicated that timber sales were economic, the numbers were skewed by the fact that the value of a standing tree was considered nothing. On the accounting ledger, a tree was worthless as wildlife habitat, a sequesterer of carbon, or a place for recreation. Half the water of eleven western states originates on national forest land, but the forests' value in protecting that water supply went unrecognized (and still does). The sale of federal timber was considered "economic" if the receipts simply paid for administering the sale and building the required roads. But rather than assets, those roads have proven to be liabilities causing landslides, erosion, loss of fisheries, and property destruction.

Hard-pressed to defend their case, supporters of the industrial subsidies linked them to the economy of logging communities. But, while logging increased dramatically in the 1980s, the number of industry jobs was cut by thirty thousand in the Northwest alone owing to mechanization and exports. The industry shipped virtually all the logs cut on private land to Asia, and the milling jobs went with them.

Moved to action at the top, Forest Service Chief Dale Robertson announced in 1992 a shift in agency policy from wholesale logging to "ecosystem management." But little actually changed to reduce the inflated cut, conserve watersheds, or protect roadless areas and endangered species.

In Oregon and Washington, the greatest of all temperate forests were cut until only 10 percent of the original old-growth stood. Going beyond the traditional appeals for recreation, scenery, and heritage, ecologists and forest enthusiasts recognized the biological values of old trees. The eminent biologist E. O. Wilson had pointed out that some ecosystems can lose 90 percent of their habitat and still retain half their biodiversity, but beyond that point a sudden collapse of the entire system occurs. With that in mind, forest activists geared up to save every remaining acre of big trees, and the spotted owl became the lightning rod for controversy after the U.S. Fish and Wildlife Service had declared it a threatened species in 1990. A cultural battle for the soul of the Pacific Northwest ensued when timber workers—who fell into line behind the mill owners—battled "tree huggers" in a conflict of public opinion, lawsuits, and civil disobedience.

Seeking to solve the impasse through compromise by both sides, President Bill Clinton in 1994 adopted a Northwest Forest Plan, protecting 70 percent of the scarce remaining uncut forest and leaving the rest—a substantial 1.4 million acres—open to logging.

By the mid-1990s, with President Clinton's Forest Service appointees in charge, logging on national forests nationwide dropped to one-third the blatantly unsustainable rate of the 1980s—to roughly its level in 1950 before the industrial-political complex had captured the agency.

Forest Service Chief Mike Dombeck took ecosystem recognition to new heights in 1998 when he called for a moratorium—and later a ban—on new road-building inside the fifty-nine million acres of national forest that were still road-free. Pointing out a staggering backlog of 8.4 billion dollars in maintenance needs on the 386,000 miles of already existing Forest Service roads, Dombeck declared, "The agency is now returning to our roots. The 1891 legislation establishing the Forest Service stated that watershed protection was central to our mission. Now, the health of our watersheds is again going to be first and foremost in our work. Fifty years from now we won't be remembered for the resources we developed, but for what we protected." This was a historic turning point for the agency.

But on the pendulum of politics, forest management swung back when President George W. Bush appointed the former executive director of the American Forest and Paper Association—an industry lobbying group—to oversee the Forest Service. The administration proceeded to unravel as much of the Clinton-era reforms as it could.

The industry, however, suffered under criticism for subsidies and also found that its pitch about jobs was less credible with all the exports and automation. The old messages weren't working, so the industry announced a new one disingenuously called "forest health." Pointing to burned areas and tracts overrun with low-grade timber that grew in the wake of earlier logging, corporate spokesmen argued that the best thing for the forest was to cut it down, or at least to "salvage" trees after fires occurred. Worsening fires had indeed killed trees, but the industry's representatives in Congress ludicrously defined salvage material to include live trees "associated" with dead ones. Ecologists were quick to point out that tracts with old trees and their shading canopies actually retard fires, and that the young, thick, even-aged stands resulting from clearcuts exacerbate the blazes, but science failed to carry the day, and virgin forests scarcely touched by flames were logged under the salvage stratagem. Legal appeals by environmental groups and the governors of West Coast states, however, prevented the most extreme Bush-era measures from gaining traction.

While national politics influenced the fate of public forests in the West, a battle over private industrial woodlands also heated up in the 1990s.

Anachronistic to the settled East, the northern forest near the Canadian border still stretches largely unbroken by development from the Atlantic to central New York. Here the timber industry owns thirteen million acres—half the region—and has re-harvested frequently for pulpwood. While the rate of cutting used to leave large expanses without roads, logging in the 1980s had accelerated with behemoth tree-cutting equipment as efficient as wheat combines. "Beauty strips" of several hundred feet along public roads and major rivers were sometimes spared, but this did little to mute ecological damage, and deceived no one who saw the disabled forest from an airplane.

AMERICAN ELM with HEMLOCK at Murray Run, north of Williamsport, Pennsylvania

This magnificent elm was alive in 1977, but it died just a year later of Dutch elm disease, brought to America by a bark beetle from Europe and a fungus likely originating in Asia. Nearly all elms in America were killed, but some resistant individuals have been found, and seeds from them are now being planted with hopes of reestablishing this splendid tree.

Cutting at this massive scale was devastating to threatened species that need larger swatches of forest, including the Blackburnian warbler, ovenbird, and colorful American redstart. In northern New England, populations of three-quarters of the woodland songbirds dropped during the clearcutting spree of the 1980s. Unsung animals such as the pine marten and fisher were just as threatened as the spotted owl in the West but went unnoticed because of a largely hands-off approach to protecting endangered species on private land.

On top of the over-harvest problem, the prospect of even greater upset surfaced when corporations began to sell off recently logged acreage for vacation homes. The liquidation pattern was abetted by a turnover of title: Many traditional logging companies sold out to financial conglomerates having no history or aptitude for forest management, nor concern for people working in the industry. Loggers got laid-off, and prime wildlife habitat along streams and lakes became ground zero in a new vacation-home subdivision boom.

To address these problems, a Northern Forest Alliance of thirty nonprofit groups worked with the legislatures and the courts, seeking better management of the remaining forest, and by 2008, the worst forms of clearcutting had been reduced. Several large land conservancies also stepped in to acquire whatever land and easements they could. In 2006, for example, the Conservation Fund bought development rights to 312,000 acres from a single industrial owner. The Nature Conservancy calculated that core reserves of twenty-five thousand acres have already been established at twenty-seven state parks, nature preserves, and similar sites across the northern forest, but that a million acres of additional safeguarded land are needed to link those reserves together in an ecologically meaningful way with protected corridors. The challenge remains to do this.

While forest issues are often portrayed as a choice between wood products and a healthy environment, scientists and foresters today recognize that if the timber industry is to continue logging, it needs to steward healthy forest ecosystems, from the soil up to the air. And ample evidence shows that good logging and functioning ecosystems can indeed coexist.

For example, the Baskahegan Company is one of a proliferating group of timber operators that are reforming the way logging is done. It cuts lightly, and in small, variable tracts, with minimum soil disturbance. While larger companies that clearcut depend on herbicides and costly replanting, this one leaves trees of varying ages—an economic way to allow natural regermination. Rather than sell for development, the company granted easements to the state and banned development in five-hundred-foot buffers along streams. As reported in *The Northern Forest*, owner Roger Milliken Jr. stated that his business "has learned that its best interests lie with the best interests of the forest." Progressive work by stewards such as Milliken offers hope for at least some of the northern woodlands of the future.

The fate of forests in the Northeast and West reflects much about the way we treat trees and forests everywhere. Reforms now underway should spare much of the small remaining acreage of old-growth—an issue that has preoccupied forest protection efforts since their start in the nineteenth century. Questions involving management of the replacement forest are now primed to receive needed attention, and responsible foresters are showing that new ways of logging can be profitable. On the forefront of this movement, ecologist Jerry Franklin at the University of Washington promotes "new forestry," allowing some trees to be cut but sparing broken snags for wildlife, leaving limbs and debris on the ground to rot and fertilize, and avoiding the erosion of roads, bulldozing, and log dragging. "Wholistic" forest management, as described by forester Herb Hammond in the anthology *Ecoforestry*, recognizes that we need to "zone" broad forest regions by identifying core areas that must be preserved for biological diversity, by protecting corridors such as riparian frontage for wildlife migration, and by limiting logging to methods that safeguard soil and streams.

For the past three centuries, logging has transformed the face of America's woodlands, but even greater changes have followed after the timber was cut. Every forest is dependent on good soil and air, but as a result of careless logging, the soil that the trees require has been diminished. Meanwhile, air pollution, including acid rain and ozone, has limited the trees' ability to resist disease, and one species after another is now struck down by exotic pests, as I saw with the hemlocks.

From the time of the first white settlement until the twentieth century, the only tree to go extinct in the wild was the elegant white-blossomed Franklinia, in 1803. The next passing was not until the chestnut's near demise in the early 1900s. But now exotic insects, fungi, and blights are diminishing many key species—not just the hemlocks and beeches, but also the ashes, sugar maples, and several white pine species in both the East and West. The beautiful butternut that my father pointed out to me as a child in the Allegheny Mountains has become the first tree named as a candidate for the endangered species list. Flowering dogwoods are dying in large numbers from a fungal disease called anthracnose. The pandemic stems from air pollution and weakened ecosystems once the soil is diminished, the community of microbes disturbed, and the chain of plant and wildlife dependencies broken.

Acid rain invades forests of the Northeast where clouds with the pH of vinegar settle in for a hundred days a year. The sulfuric and nitric acid comes from power plants, cars, commercial fertilizers, and other products of the petroleum age. Unpolluted rain has a pH of 5.6, but forests in a broad belt from New York to Tennessee test at a corrosive 4.2.

The acid destroys waxy surfaces of leaves and makes open wounds that are vulnerable to fungi and bacteria. Settling on the soil of the forest floor, acid rain dissolves aluminum, nickel, zinc, and lead in toxic doses, which are then taken up by trees. Acid rain and frequent logging also leach calcium from soil, and could result in a 50 percent reduction of forest biomass in 120 years according to a September 1989 article in *Environmental Management*. This troubling trend directly conflicts with the need to combat global warming by growing more trees.

Excessive ozone in the lower atmosphere is a separate but related problem caused by pollution from burning oil, gas, and coal. Resulting leaf damage restricts photosynthesis. Fifty-five percent of the trees in the southern Sierra Nevada—including giant sequoia seedlings—have been affected, and many of them killed, by ozone. Ninety different plant species in the Smoky Mountains of the Southeast suffer from ozone pollution. In its 1999 report, *Forest Resources of the United States*, the Forest Service indicated that nationally tree mortality had increased 24 percent between 1986 and 1991. Mortality of deciduous trees jumped a shocking 37 percent. The Lucy Braun Association of the central Appalachians reported that trees are dying at two to four times the expected rate. Areas of greatest mortality coincided with the worst acid rain and ozone. Some reform efforts—by California for example—have led to decreased air pollution per capita. Yet population growth continues to soar, causing dramatic increases in overall car and energy use. The resulting global warming upsets the climatic balance that whole forests depend upon, and it favors pests such as the mountain pine beetle, which is currently killing an unprecedented 90 percent of the lodgepole pines in some areas of the Rocky Mountains.

While soil damage from logging, air pollution, and global warming stand as formidable threats to forests, other problems also diminish the woodland beauty and forest ecosystems of our country. Affecting every region, the invasion of exotic (non-native) plants—from tamarisk on floodplains of the Southwest, to scotch broom in the Northwest, to Chinese privet and kudzu in the East—preempts the space needed by native trees. In California, majestic valley oaks fail to regenerate, in part because exotic weeds mat the soil. Threatening woodlands everywhere, a whole new round of invasives are feared because of increased imports of wood that began in the 1990s. Poorly understood, scarcely monitored, and inadequately regulated, log imports from Asia and the tropics pose the specter of ecological disaster under the guise of globalism and could wreak new havoc in American forests.

Another reason for the collapse of forest ecosystems has been our misguided compulsion to suppress all forest fires. Before white settlement, frequent lightening-caused fires walked through the woods, burning fallen limbs and brush, keeping the understory open and parklike, and encouraging grasses and wildlife forage. Native Americans also burned large tracts frequently. The crowns of tall trees, such as ponderosa pines, rose beyond the reach of flames because the frequent low blazes cleaned up the brush and deadfall at the bases of the trunks. But, by spending billions of dollars to protect commercial timber and country homes built in harm's way, we've suppressed natural fires for a century. Now, without the thinning action of frequent low-level flames, a tangle of unhealthy forests are the norm. Prone to disease, these thickets are tinderboxes for superheated blazes. This problem is aggravated by global warming; because of it, the threats of fires are worse, and the chances of recovery are less. In 1999 the General Accounting Office warned that forty-five million forest acres were primed to burn. In spite of firefighters' best efforts, infernos in the shaggy, logged-over forests of today escape containment and rage out of control with blast-furnace intensity rather than the low-level kindling typical in the natural fire regime of old. One solution to this problem is to thin small trees, allow the large ones to grow, and burn in a controlled way that simulates the conditions of the past. Some land managers are trying to do this, but the scope of the problem is enormous.

Once logged or burned, forests may or may not grow back. But once developed, they never recover. At low elevations, where statuesque oaks dotted California grasslands in an artistic savanna, urban sprawl now gobbles twenty thousand to sixty thousand acres of woodlands a year. Nationwide, one million acres of forest are converted to urban use annually. Trying to stem this loss, and reminding us that one tree can absorb up to fifty pounds of carbon from the atmosphere each year, American Forests sponsors an initiative to regreen cities, suburbs, and burned areas. The National Arbor Day Foundation likewise champions tree planting.

The loss of wild forests to land development can be avoided through the purchase of woodlands by land conservancies. The largest among these—the Nature Conservancy, Trust for Public Land, and Conservation Fund—acquire extensive tracts of open space each year. More than a thousand smaller land trusts do similar work. Beyond these efforts, good planning, such as clustering new housing development rather than allowing large-lot sprawl, can delay the march of suburbia. However, as long as the American population doubles every fifty-six years, as it's doing currently, even the best planning will do little to stop the eventual conversion of forests to suburbs.

To cope with the ominous threats to our forests, citizens nationwide are acting on seven essential fronts:

First, environmentalists continue to press for protection of the few remaining ancient forests by designating federal lands as wilderness, or through government or land trust acquisition of the best remaining old-growth on private land.

Second, interest in restoring mature forests is increasing. Ecologists say that if trees are allowed to grow, forests can again evolve into natural communities of complex and resilient diversity, and old-growth conditions can be recovered. Links are also needed between protected areas for migration, feeding, and genetic exchange of wildlife. Ecologist Robert Zahner has recommended that 80 percent of our eastern national forest acreage be reserved for restoring old-growth (this is still only 7 percent of all eastern forests).

Third, the way owners manage private woodlots, industrial tracts, or public land is determining much about the health of whole forest ecosystems. The problems of soil erosion, road-induced landslides, and invasion of exotic species after a forest is cut are receiving closer attention. The "new forestry" advocated by ecologist Jerry Franklin can do much to mitigate the harmful effects of commercial logging.

Fourth, everybody uses wood, and some are recognizing that we can be more efficient. Consumption now increases by 1 percent per year—identical to the rate of population growth. Forty-four percent of the wood we use is for construction and 27 percent for paper. Yet we fail to effectively recycle both. For example, two-fifths of our landfill space is consumed by paper, virtually all of which could be recycled. By improving efficiency, total wood consumption in the United States can reasonably be halved, according to the Worldwatch Institute (assuming no population increase).

Fifth, some people are trying to address the invasion of exotic species. This requires tighter controls on incoming vectors, research about resistance to pests, and labor-intensive initiatives to eradicate invasive species. Some managers are valiantly stopping the exotics at the borders of particular state parks, national parks, other public lands, and land-trust preserves, but the larger problem is virtually ignored across most of the country.

Sixth, because land development is slated to convert twenty-three million acres of forest land to suburban development by 2050, according to the Conservation Fund and the U.S. Forest Service, organizations addressing land use encourage clustered development and strive to conserve the best forest land, preferably by acquisition as open space.

Seventh, people increasingly recognize that the forest's larger life-support system requires urgent attention. Acid rain, ozone, and global warming all need to be reduced if our forests are to survive as sources of life and regulators of vital hydrologic, climatic, and ecological processes. Reforestation is needed in order to sequester carbon, and fossil fuel use must be reduced to curb global warming. Because 40 percent of our oil powers automobiles, better fuel-efficiency standards are essential.

LONGLEAF PINES near Thomasville, Georgia

Once covering much of the South, longleaf pines were logged for their valuable timber until only small, isolated tracts remained. Birds such as the red-cockaded woodpecker, which need the large pines for construction of nesting cavities, are threatened because of the trees' demise. Some stands are now being restored by frequent burning of the understory. In private ownership, the Wade Tract, shown here, is one of the finest longleaf forests.

A 40 percent improvement—eminently feasible—would reduce the current production of carbon dioxide by half, provided the number of cars and the mileage driven remain stable.

But the number of cars doesn't remain stable, and in that regard, a few far-sighted organizations work on the final, and perhaps most crucial in this list of reforms—population stabilization. They argue that, no matter what else we do, forests and other open spaces will constantly be lost to development if we have unlimited population growth, and trees will be harvested unsustainably to meet ever increasing demands. Even the most optimistic goals for improving efficiency and reducing per capita consumption will eventually be nullified by unlimited population growth. These organizations maintain that the plague of global warming will not be reversed as long as the population of America—which causes a grossly disproportionate share of greenhouse gas production—continues to increase, especially at the current rate of doubling in far less than a lifetime. This high rate of population growth results primarily from immigration now occurring in record numbers. New immigrants and their children will account for 66 to 85 percent of the population increase to the year 2050 according to Census Bureau data. Unless the difficult issue of population growth is addressed fairly and responsibly, there is little hope for the long-term protection, restoration, or sustainability of forests in America.

THE MODERN PROBLEMS OF forests can be overwhelming in their complexity. Yet today, people everywhere are pushing for reform and taking new responsibility for their woodlands. Many organizations recognize that a central issue for the future of forests is no longer one of environmentalists battling with loggers, and no longer one of saving a single woodland species such as the spotted owl. Rather, the issue is the health of whole forests.

"Forest health" is not just industrial spin to speciously rationalize logging but rather an ecological condition that allows woodlands to thrive with a full complement of native plants and animals. Forest health means having plantlife that builds soil, protects it from erosion, and moderates the effects of floods, droughts, and the weather. Healthy forests should provide for people's needs without losing the ability to provide for those needs in the future.

With a large membership and a prestigious history, the organization American Forests addresses issues such as reforestation, urban ecosystems, and community-supported management of forests. Large land conservancies and a plethora of smaller ones try to buy the most important wooded groves to spare them from development. Large conservation groups such as the National Wildlife Federation and the Natural Resources Defense Council lobby for improvements in the way our forests are managed. Smaller groups, such as the California Oak Foundation, focus on specific families of trees. The Save the Redwoods League has funded the protection of many redwood groves.

Most forest groups are dedicated to specific areas. A model in this regard, the Society for the Protection of New Hampshire Forests has been active since 1901. The Southern Appalachian Forest Coalition represents many groups, and the Eastern Native Tree Society works throughout its wide region. The Heartwood Forest Council brings activists together from across the East, Midwest, and South. Oregon Wild fights to save the remaining 10 percent of ancient forests in the Northwest. Near the Pacific Coast, the Siskiyou Project has adopted the world's most diverse collection of conifers as a forest that must be tended with respect and care. These are just a few among hundreds of fine organizations that deserve the support of everybody who cares about trees and forests.

Moved by the power of trees to provide for life, to inspire our minds, and to delight our spirits, people who value woodlands all across America are recognizing that the fate of our forests and the fate of ourselves are one and the same.

SEEING THE TREES AND THE FOREST

FORESTS ARE KEEPERS OF soil, water, and climate. They are home to many people and also to wildlife. Trees produce the air we breathe. They make the wood we use. We need them, and they are beautiful.

While the challenges of the forests are many, and the losses are at once heartbreaking and outraging, the pictures in this book celebrate what remains. Each photo was taken, and this book was created, with the belief that seeing and understanding our trees and woodlands will inspire us to care for our land and to restore intrinsic qualities to the forests of the future.

The rewards of better stewardship are as compelling as the life force that was still evident in every woods I saw, from mangroves clutching oysters in their roots at the Gulf of Mexico, to America's westernmost trees, gripping the ground tenaciously where Alaska curves out across the north Pacific. I went seeking those outermost trees, and eventually spotted them from a windy mountaintop on Kodiak Island. In the sheltered valley below, a hearty Sitka spruce pioneered glaciated soil where great bears still roam. Like that evergreen vanguard in the far northwest, some seven hundred kinds of trees still grace our continent from one seashore to the other, and like the Sitka spruce, each species is a natural work of art.

One of the most extraordinary but rare trees is the Port Orford cedar. This great conifer has suffered a trajectory of loss much like the chestnut, owing to a fungus introduced from Asia. But biologists and foresters found resistant cedars, gathered their cones, and propagated their seeds. Just this spring, in my own backyard near the coast of southern Oregon, I planted disease-resistant cedars. With hope, I watch them grow.

With similar hope, my wife Ann and I work through a local conservation group trying to reverse shortsighted decisions that affect great tracts of woodlands here at the edge of the Pacific. After a lot of persuasion by many people through many years, the U.S. Forest Service in our area now plans to thin crowded plantations of trees without cutting the scarce old-growth that persists. We think that Congress will soon safeguard the Copper Salmon Wilderness. Ann and I take part in local planning and try to stop the sprawl that unnecessarily chews away the forest. As to the greater challenges—air pollution, global warming, and an American population expanding with no limits in sight—we support larger organizations that are engaged in reform. We back politicians who act to correct the tragic course we are on, and we oppose those who do not. We do all of this with a vision of the land in mind—a vision we can actually see, in real life, in some of the forests around us. I have tried to capture a part of that vision in this book, recognizing the forest as a place of natural beauty and wonder. It's a place we all need, no less than we need food to eat and water to drink.

Some of the news is good and a lot of it is bad, but standing at this uncertain edge of time, I still enjoy the shade of the woods, as people have surely done for the millennia. I still smile at the sound of wind in the branches high above, at the smell of springtime flowers on dogwoods or laurels, at the taste of a hazelnut or serviceberry popped into my mouth as I travel down the path I've chosen. When I'm in the woods, I don't want to miss a thing. I try to notice the details at my feet and also the big view, far away. Seeing the trees as well as the forest, I'm still amazed when green leaves appear in the spring and when they turn brilliant red in autumn, and I'm still gratified to know that some forests remain as wild places, nourishing life, just as they have done for all the ages.

OLD RAG MOUNTAIN, Virginia
Tuliptrees reach for the sky in Shenandoah National Park.

BEECH TREES, **Ricketts Glen, Pennsylvania**

Young beech trees shine with autumn color along Kitchen Creek in northcentral Pennsylvania.

PACIFIC DOGWOOD, WESTERN HEMLOCK, and MAPLES, Cascade Mountains, Washington

With the green and flowering promise of spring, vine and bigleaf maples accompany a Pacific dogwood within a deep forest of western hemlocks and Douglas-firs.

Overleaf: PONDEROSA and LODGEPOLE PINES, Sierra Nevada, California

A light snowfall covers these pines in their rocky landscape near the North Fork of the Stanislaus River.

FLOWERING DOGWOOD, Bent of the River Audubon Preserve, Southbury, Connecticut

Bursting with blooms in May, a dogwood tree flowers in front of a large red oak and other hardwoods above the Pomperaug River.

VALLEY OAK in the Eastman Lake National Recreation Area, California
With the sun beaming at the distant crest of the Sierra Nevada, a valley oak spreads its durable limbs over a grassland savanna in the foothills. This is one of few sizeable valley oak savannas in public ownership.

PAPER BIRCHES and other Hardwoods near the Brule River, Wisconsin

Lichens cover the white trunks of paper birches, red and sugar maples have turned red and yellow, and a few northern red oaks rise above bracken ferns and big-leaved asters.

RED MAPLE near Lake Superior, Wisconsin
A cluster of red maples bathes in low autumn sunlight. Yellow birches are turning from green to yellow in the colorful understory.

WESTERN WHITE PINE and MOUNTAIN HEMLOCK south of Donner Pass, California
A western white pine stands tall at the crest of the Sierra Nevada while an early-summer sunset glows across the range's western slope.

SOURCES AND FURTHER READING

To find my photo locations, I relied on natural history guidebooks, state park descriptions from the Internet, word of mouth, files that I've accumulated for decades, and a lifetime of traveling experience. I highly recommend DeLorme atlases for each state, which include lists of natural areas with notes that identify exceptional public forests.

The quarterly magazine *American Forests* is a fine publication with a variety of articles, including good coverage of current issues by Jane Braxton Little. The Forest History Society, based in Durham, North Carolina, is the ultimate resource for the history of our forests. *Forest Voice*, published by the Native Forest Council in Eugene, Oregon, covers the cutting edge of controversy in efforts for forest management reform, especially in the Northwest, and *The Northern Forest Forum*, based in Lancaster, New Hampshire, fills this role for the Northeast. Many professional foresters depend on the *Journal of Forestry*, published by the Society of American Foresters, for information.

Few other modern photo books with an explicit focus on forests have been published, but I recommend the wonderfully illustrated *Enduring Forests*, covering the Northwest, and *Tree*, which shows James Balog's amazing perspectives of "champion" trees made possible with mosaics assembled from a digital camera.

The books below informed my writing and offer a wealth of information about trees and forests to anyone who wants to learn more. I've included easy-to-find materials and offer short annotations.

Agee, James K. *Fire Ecology of Pacific Northwest Forests*. Washington, D.C.: Island Press, 1993. A scientific account of northwestern forests and fire.

Alverson, William S., Walter Kuhlmann, and Donald M. Waller. *Wild Forests: Conservation Biology and Public Policy*. Washington, D.C.: Island Press, 1994. A survey of the science and policy issues.

Aplet, Gregory H. et al, eds. *Defining Sustainable Forestry*. Washington, D.C.: Island Press, 1993. The need to transform forestry with an ecosystem approach. Includes amounts of old-growth remaining and policy changes of the Forest Service.

Arno, Stephen F. and Ramona P. Hammerly. *Timberline: Mountain and Arctic Forest Frontiers*. Seattle, WA: The Mountaineers, 1984. Natural history and fine sketches of high-elevation forests. See also Arno and Hammerly's *Northwest Trees*, 2007.

Ayers, Harvard, Jenny Hager, and Charles E. Little, eds. *An Appalachian Tragedy: Air Pollution and Tree Death in the Eastern Forests of North America*. San Francisco, CA: Sierra Club Books, 1998. Air pollution and forests.

Balog, James. *Tree: A New Vision of the American Forest*. New York, NY: Sterling, 2004. Photos from multiple digital images that illustrate the full height and breadth of large trees.

Belsky, Joy. "Incoming: The Ecological Risks of Log Imports," *Wild Forest Review*, August 1994. The problems of log imports.

Berger, John J. *Understanding Forests*. San Francisco, CA: Sierra Club Books, 1998. An overview of the ecology, history, and future of forests, especially on public land.

Best, Constance and Laurie A. Wayburn. *America's Private Forests: Status and Stewardship*. Washington, D.C.: Island Press, 2001. The status and conservation of private forests.

Bolgiano, Chris. *The Appalachian Forest*. Harrisburg, PA: Stackpole, 1998. A natural and cultural history of the eastern forest.

Bosworth, Barbara. *Trees: National Champions*. Cambridge, MA: MIT Press, 2006. Fine black-and-white photos of the largest trees, which are mostly in settled areas.

Brockman, Frank C. *Trees of North America*. New York, NY: Golden Press, 1986. Identification guide.

Caras, Roger. *The Forest*. Boston, MA: Houghton Mifflin, 1979. Eminently readable natural history of a western forest.

The Conservation Fund and the U.S. Forest Service, State and Private Forestry, Northeastern Area. *The State of Chesapeake Forests*. Arlington, VA: The Fund, c. 2006, booklet. The forest's importance to water quality.

Constantz, George. *Hollows, Peepers, and Highlanders: An Appalachian Mountain Ecology*. Missoula, MT: Mountain Press, 1994. The ecology of the Appalachians, including acid rain's effect on soil.

Davis, Mary Byrd. *Eastern Old-Growth Forests: Prospects for Rediscovery and Recovery*. Washington, D.C.: Island Press, 1996. Essays on the science and geography of eastern forests, including Robert Zahner estimate of restoration needed.

Devall, Bill. *Clearcut: The Tragedy of Industrial Forestry*. San Francisco, CA: Sierra Club Books and Earth Island Press, 1993. A remarkable book of photos showing clearcutting in North America, with text about the problems and solutions. Superb essays by Chris Maser, Alan Drengson, Herb Hammond, Reed Noss,

Felice Pace, Mitch Lansky, Jan Wilder-Thomas, Dave Foreman, Warnick Fox, Edward Grumbine, Orville Camp, and others.

Dietrich, William. *The Final Forest: The Battle for the Last Great Trees of the Pacific Northwest*. New York, NY: Penguin, 1992. A journalist's account of the timber controversies of the 1980s on the Olympic Peninsula.

Dobbs, David and Richard Ober. *The Northern Forest*. White River Junction, VT: Chelsea Green, 1995. Controversies surrounding the northern forest.

Dregson, Alan and Duncan Taylor, eds. *Ecoforestry: The Art and Science of Sustainable Forest Use*. Gabriola Island, B.C.: New Society Publishers, 1997. Essays on new approaches to forestry.

Durbin, Kathie. *Tree Huggers: Victory, Defeat & Renewal in the Northwest Ancient Forest Campaign*. Seattle, WA: The Mountaineers, 1996. The definitive history of the struggle to preserve the last old-growth in the Northwest.

E Magazine, "Parks as Lungs," November 2001. Ability of trees to filter air pollution.

Federer, Anthony, et al. "Long-term depletion of calcium and other nutrients in eastern U.S. forests." *Environmental Management*, September 1989. Loss of calcium and forests owing to logging and air pollution.

Feininger, Andreas. *Trees*. New York, NY: Rizzoli, 1991 (original edition, 1968). A vintage photo book with text about trees in America.

Heinrich, Bernd. *The Trees in My Forest*. New York, NY: HarperCollins, 1997. A biologist's and artist's excellent description of trees and how they live.

Hill, Julia Butterfly. *The Legacy of Luna: The Story of a Tree, a Woman, and the Struggle to Save the Redwoods*. San Francisco, CA: Harper, 2000. Amazing story of a young woman's determination to save a tree.

Hirt, Paul. *A Conspiracy of Optimism: Management of the National Forests Since World War Two*. Lincoln, NE: University of Nebraska Press, 1994. An environmental historian's narrative about national forests.

Johnston, Verna R. *California Forests and Woodlands*. Berkeley, CA: University of California Press, 1994. A fine natural history.

Keaton, Glenn. *The Life of an Oak: An Intimate Portrait*. Berkeley, CA: Heyday Books, 1998. Photos and text including tree physiology.

Kerr, Andy. *Oregon Wild: Endangered Forest Wilderness*. Portland, OR: Oregon Natural Resources Council, 2004. A remarkable compendium about wild forests in Oregon.

Kirk, Ruth, ed. *The Enduring Forests: Northern California, Oregon, Washington, British Columbia, and Southeast Alaska*. Seattle, WA: The Mountaineers, 1996. An exquisite book about the Northwest.

Kohm, Kathryn A. and Jerry F. Franklin, eds. *Creating a Forestry for the 21st Century*. Washington, D.C.: Island Press, 1997. New forestry and improved methods of logging.

Langston, Nancy. *Forest Dreams, Forest Nightmares: The Paradox of Old Growth in the Inland West*. Seattle, WA: University of Washington Press, 1995. History of the mismanagement of forests in the Blue Mountains of Oregon.

Lansky, Mitch. *Beyond the Beauty Strip: Saving What's Left of Our Forests*. Gardiner, ME: Tilbury House, 1992. A hard-hitting exposé about the destruction of the northern forests of Maine, with relevance to industrial forestry everywhere.

Little, Charles. E. *The Dying of the Trees: The Pandemic in America's Forests*. New York, NY: Viking, 1995. An extraordinary account of the modern problems of blight, disease, and air pollution; perhaps the most important book on this list.

Luoma, Jon R. *The Hidden Forest*. New York, NY: Henry Holt, 1999. Narrative science writing about the Northwest.

Maser, Chris. *From the Forest to the Sea: The Ecology of Wood in Streams, Estuaries, and Oceans*. Delray Beach, FL: St. Lucie Press, 1994. The importance of decomposing trees to aquatic systems. See also *Forest Primeval*.

Natural Resources Defense Council, "Forever Forests," *Amicus Journal*, September 1997. Waste of wood and paper, and recycling potential.

The Nature Conservancy. *Determining the Size of Eastern Forest Reserves*. Boston, MA: The Conservancy, 2004, brochure. The opportunity to connect forest reserves in the Northeast.

Norse, Elliott A. *Ancient Forests of the Pacific Northwest*. Washington, D.C.: Island Press, 1990. Ecological overview of northwestern forests and the threats to them.

Noss, Reed, ed. *The Redwood Forest: History, Ecology, and Conservation of the Coast Redwoods*. Washington, D.C.: Island Press, 2000. Anthology of scientific articles.

Oregon Forest Resources Institute, Oregon State University College of Forestry and Oregon Department of Forestry.

Forests, Carbon, and Climate Change. The Institute, 2006. A primer on global warming and forests.

Palmer, Tim. *California's Threatened Environment*. Washington, D.C.: Island Press, 1993. Includes two chapters about forests and oak woodlands.

———. *The Columbia*. Seattle, WA: The Mountaineers, 1997. The issues affecting forests of the Columbia basin.

Pavlik, Bruce M., et al. *Oaks of California*. Los Olivos, CA: Cachuma Press, 1991. Overview of oaks, with fine photos.

Peattie, Donald Culross. *A Natural History of Trees of Eastern and Central North America*. Boston, MA: Houghton Mifflin, 1966. This classic book offers colorful descriptions of trees. Principally a cultural history, it focuses on the uses we have made of each species.

———. *A Natural History of Western Trees*. New York, NY: Crown, 1953. See above.

Petrides, George A. and Olivia Petrides. *Western Trees* (Peterson Field Guide). Boston, MA: Houghton Mifflin, 1992. Identification guide.

Petrides, George A. and Janet Wehr. *Eastern Trees* (Peterson Field Guide). Boston, MA: Houghton Mifflin, 1988. Identification guide.

Postel, Sandra and John C. Ryan. "Reforming Forestry," *State of the World*, Lester R. Brown, ed. New York, NY: Norton, 1991. U.S. imports of lumber; source for "50 percent reduction of wood use possible in U.S."

Powell, Douglas. *Forest Resources of the United States*. Ft. Collins, CO: USDA Forest Service, Rocky Mountain Forest and Range Experiment Station, 1993. Timber mortality from air pollution.

Preston, Richard. *The Wild Trees: A Story of Passion and Daring*. New York, NY: Random House, 2007. A gripping story about big-tree climbers and ecologists who study the redwoods.

Raphael, Ray. *Tree Talk: The People and Politics of Timber*. Covelo, CA: Island Press, 1981. Excellent account of alternative approaches to logging. See also *More Tree Talk: The People, Politics, and Economics of Timber*, 1994.

Rice, Richard E. *National Forests: Policies for the Future, The Uncounted Costs of Logging*. Washington, D.C. : Wilderness Society, 1989. Analysis of subsidies.

Roberts, Paul. "The Federal Chain-Saw Massacre," *Harpers*, June 1997. Logging subsidies.

Robinson, Gordon. *The Forest and The Trees: A Guide to Excellent Forestry*. Washington, D.C.: Island Press, 1988. A path-breaking book at its time, this forester analyzes modern logging and proposes reforms.

Sundquist, Eric T. "Long-Term Aspects of Future Atmospheric CO2 and Sea-Level Change," *Sea Level Change*. Roger R. Revelle et al, eds. Washington, D.C.: National Research Council and National Academy Press, 1990. Global warming.

Suzuki, David and Wayne Grady. *Tree: A Life Story*. Vancouver, B.C.: Greystone, 2004. The story of a northwestern conifer, told by one of the finest science commentators of our time.

Tudge, Colin. *The Tree: A Natural History of What Trees Are, How They Live, and Why They Matter*. New York, NY: Crown, 2005. Descriptions of taxonomy and life processes of trees.

U.S. Department of the Interior, National Biological Service, *Our Living Resources*. Edward T. LaRoe, et al, eds. Washington, D.C.: the Service, 1995. Forests, global warming, and plants' ability to migrate.

Walker, Laurence C. *The North American Forests: Geography, Ecology, and Silviculture*. Boca Raton, FL: CRC Press, 1999. A production-oriented forester's survey, with emphasis on silviculture.

Wessels, Tom. *Reading the Forested Landscape: A Natural History of New England*. Woodstock, VT: Countryman Press, 1997. Fascinating interpretation of natural processes in the woods.

Wilkinson, Charles F. and H. Michael Anderson. *Land and Resource Planning in the National Forests*. Washington, D.C.: Island Press, 1987. History and policy of forest planning; covers the uncounted values of forests in Forest Service timber sales.

Williams, Michael. *Americans & Their Forests: A Historical Geography*. New York, NY: Cambridge University Press, 1989. History of how Americans have used their forests.

Wood, Wendell. *A Walking Guide to Oregon's Ancient Forests*. Portland, OR: Oregon Natural Resources Council, 1991. A Guide to old-growth in Oregon.

Van Pelt, Robert. *Forest Giants of the Pacific Coast*. Seattle, WA: University of Washington Press, 2002. A splendid guide to big trees in the Northwest.

Yafee, Steven Lewis. *The Wisdom of the Spotted Owl: Policy Lessons for a New Century*. Washington, D.C.: Island Press, 1994. A history of public policy regarding the spotted owl, endangered species, and forests.

ACKNOWLEDGMENTS

As MY PARTNER IN WRITING, in the woods, and in life, Ann Vileisis deserves unlimited thanks for everything. Everything. I simply could not do what I do without the brilliance, support, and love of my wife.

At Harry N. Abrams, senior editor Charles Kochman has handled my work and his job with endlessly impressive skill and indescribably good spirit. I am one fortunate writer and photographer to be associated with Charlie. Editor Sofia Gutierrez gracefully, capably, and enthusiastically guided production and fielded many problems and opportunities that arose between my manuscript and the book in your hands. Brady McNamara is the artistic genius who made my images from the real, 3-D, organic world come to life once again on flat pieces of paper. And I know that the marketing staff at Abrams will do a superb job of sending my book out into the world. Thanks, as well, to all the other fine people at Abrams.

Jim Rogers is a woodland friend in a class all by himself. Professional forester, backwoods guide, and undaunted activist for wild nature, Jim has shown me what needs to be shown to others, and he's led the fight to save what's left in our own special part of the world. Bob Webber of Slate Run, Pennsylvania, inspired me years ago to care about the forest where I lived for an important time in my life. Jerry Becker—"ecoforester"—has also offered a perspective on the woods and a lifetime of good work that's impressive to anyone who notices what he is doing through the Elk River Land Trust. I also thank Jerry for the Land Trust's planting of 250 trees that I sponsored—more than double the number that were likely needed to produce this book.

My family, including my mother, Jane Palmer May, her husband Chuck May, my brother Jim, and my sisters, Becky Schmitz and Brenda Murray, have all supported me in uncountable ways since day one. Though he died many years ago, my father, Jim Palmer, first took me to the woods, and he let me fly with my own special sense of adventure.

I happened to marry into a friendship with Marc Taylor—Ann's stepfather—who is a rare model for good living and for commitment to all that's most worthy of our time and effort. And Ann's mother, Janet Taylor, is simply the best.

Jim Britell deserves special thanks for his commitment to stop the political machine of forest destruction that he found when he first moved to southern Oregon, and to later entice Ann and me to buy the old house that he had rebuilt with grace, charm, and perfection.

Several people have read my manuscript and provided useful comments: Ann Vileisis, English professor Nat Hart, environmental educator and biodiversity aficionado Ed Grumbine, and forester Jim Rogers.

I'd be dead in my tracks, photographically speaking, if it weren't for Steve Sweringen, my camera-repair guru, reachable at the Camera Clinic in Sparks, Nevada. If you want to keep your film camera working, along with all those optically perfect old Canon lenses, Steve's the man, and he also works on digital cameras.

Like every writer out there, I've written nothing new except for what I miraculously discovered all alone (not much), and I'm deeply indebted to a hall-of-fame of others who have come this way before me. To see a list of books by writers I found helpful, if not fascinating and indispensable—see the "Sources and Further Reading" pages in this volume. At risk of redundancy, I can't help but mention again two monumental achievements: Charles E. Little's *The Dying of the Trees: The Pandemic in America's Forests*, and *Clearcut: The Tragedy of Industrial Forestry*. Don't be turned-off by the severity of these titles. Each relates stories of critical importance that I've discussed but not begun to address adequately in the limited space of this book.

Fellow photographer Beth Maynor Young has a wonderful eye and heart, and showed Ann and me some stunningly photogenic woodlands in the South. For hospitality or advice when I visited other regions, thanks to John Helland in Minnesota, Bob Banks in Wisconsin, Ken Cline at the College of the Atlantic in Maine, Jamie and Florence Williams in South Carolina and Montana, Nick and Ricia Shema in Hawaii, and Phil Spivey and Nathan Klaus—both dedicated wildlife biologists in Georgia. Jerry Franklin and Ken Bible made the University of Washington's canopy crane available so that I could look down on some very tall trees.

Arthur Davis—another natural resource pro who was trained as a forester—probably has no idea that he, long ago, taught me to look for the big picture and the pivotal point that really counts. Finally, though it's way too late, I owe special thanks to another real professional, Penn State Forestry Professor Dr. Peter Fletcher, who engaged me early in conservation and showed me that a dedicated man who loves the woods can spend a lifetime doing work that's both important to the world and joyously nourishing to the spirit.

ABOUT THE AUTHOR/PHOTOGRAPHER

TIM PALMER HAS WRITTEN nineteen books about the American landscape, rivers, conservation, and adventure travel. His 2006 book, *Rivers of America*, was published by Harry N. Abrams and features two hundred color photos of rivers nationwide. His recent book of photos and text, *Luminous Mountains: The Sierra Nevada of California*, was published in 2008 by Heyday Books and the Yosemite Association.

Tim's book of text and color photos about wilderness in California, *California Wild*, won the Benjamin Franklin Award as the best book on nature and the environment in 2004. *The Heart of America: Our Landscape, Our Future* won the Independent Publisher's Book Award as the best essay and travel book in 2000. *The Columbia* won the National Outdoor Book Award in 1998. Tim wrote the text for the Yosemite Association's *Yosemite: The Promise of Wildness*, which received the Director's Award in 1997 from the National Park Service as the best book about a national park.

Recognizing his accumulated contributions in writing, photography, and activism, the organization American Rivers gave Tim its first Lifetime Achievement Award in 1988. Perception, Inc. honored him as America's River Conservationist of the Year in 2000, and in 2002 California's Friends of the River recognized him with its highest honor, the Peter Behr Award. *Paddler* magazine named him one of the ten greatest river conservationists of our time, and in 2000 included him as one of the "100 greatest paddlers of the century." In 2005 Tim received the Distinguished Alumni Award from the College of Arts and Architecture at The Pennsylvania State University.

Photographing the forests of America, Tim has traveled extensively by foot and on skis, in his canoe, and in his well-equipped van. He frequently speaks and gives slide shows at universities, outdoor clubs, workshops, and conferences nationwide, and can be reached at tim@timpalmer.org.

Large TULIPTREES at the Joyce Kilmer Memorial Forest, North Carolina

INDEX

Page numbers in italics refer to illustrations.

BIGLEAF MAPLE, Prairie Creek Redwoods State Park, California

EDITOR
Sofia Gutiérrez

DESIGNER
Brady McNamara

PRODUCTION MANAGER
Alison Gervais

LIBRARY OF CONGRESS CATALOGING-IN-PUBLICATION DATA
Palmer, Tim, 1948-
Trees and forests of America / by Tim Palmer.
p. cm.
ISBN 978-0-8109-7294-0
1. Photography of trees. 2. Palmer, Tim, 1948- 3. Trees—United States—Pictorial works. 4. Forests and forestry—United States—Pictorial works. I. Title.
TR726.T7P35 2008
779'.30973—dc22 2008002985

Printed and bound in China
10 9 8 7 6 5 4 3 2 1

harry n. abrams, inc.
a subsidiary of La Martinière Groupe
115 West 18th Street
New York, NY 10011
www.hnabooks.com